"A mix of insightful theology, historical research, and personal narrative, this book is necessary reading for anyone who seeks justice in the church. Hardwick highlights the history of ableism and racism in US churches and invites us to a joy-filled reversal of the shame that comes from worshiping these idols."

—**Amy Kenny**, director, Disability Cultural Center, Georgetown University; author of *My Body Is Not a Prayer Request*

"Ableism has been a fixture in our society for far too long, determining which bodies are deserving and which ones are not. It has also influenced architectural designs that dictate who can occupy public spaces—upholding views that trample on the dignity of the disabled community. Hardwick draws a connection between race and disability and what we must do to dismantle a hierarchy of bodies to achieve a more just society in our churches, communities, and the world. As he says, 'disability is not a dirty word,' and I join him in asserting that the time to resist believing this is now."

—**Terence Lester**, founder of Love Beyond Walls; author of *All God's Children, I See You*, and *When We Stand*

"Lamar Hardwick provides a sweeping review of the way historical and theological ableism upholds American Christian racism. Grounded in his own embodied experience and pastoral perspective, Hardwick has given us a book that is relatable, persuasive, and perhaps most important, constructive. He not only levels incisive critique but also shows how embracing disability theology helps confront the shameful underside of American Christianity, heralding a fuller vision of God and humanity."

—**Erin Raffety**, researcher, Princeton Theological Seminary; lecturer, Princeton University

HOW ABLEISM FUELS RACISM

Dismantling the Hierarchy of Bodies in the Church

Lamar Hardwick

BrazosPress

a division of Baker Publishing Group
Grand Rapids, Michigan

© 2024 by J. Lamar Hardwick

Published by Brazos Press
a division of Baker Publishing Group
Grand Rapids, Michigan
www.BrazosPress.com

Printed in the United States of America

Library of Congress Cataloging-in-Publication Data
Names: Hardwick, Lamar, 1978– author.
Title: How ableism fuels racism : dismantling the hierarchy of bodies in the church / Lamar Hardwick.
Description: Grand Rapids, Michigan : Brazos Press, a division of Baker Publishing Group, [2024] | Includes bibliographical references.
Identifiers: LCCN 2023028482 | ISBN 9781587436123 (paperback) | ISBN 9781587436284 (casebound) | ISBN 9781493444984 (ebook)
Subjects: LCSH: Disabilities—Religious aspects—Christianity. | Discrimination against people with disabilities. | Race relations—Religious aspects—Christianity.
Classification: LCC BV4460 .H278 2024 | DDC 261.8/321—dc23/eng/20230819
LC record available at https://lccn.loc.gov/2023028482

The author is represented by the literary agency of Credo Communications, LLC, www.credocommunications.net.

Baker Publishing Group publications use paper produced from sustainable forestry practices and post-consumer waste whenever possible.

24   25   26   27   28   29   30   7   6   5   4   3   2   1

CONTENTS

A NOTE ABOUT DISABILITY LANGUAGE

The field of disability study is an ever-growing and organic area of interest that continues to evolve and change. This is also true of the field of disability theology. Disability studies and disability theology are distinctive approaches to helping society better understand the role of disability, chronic illness, and human limitation in the face of a changing culture.

One of the hallmarks of an evolving culture is the fluid nature of its language. Ideas and terms that were once socially accepted sometimes become outdated. Then there are times when terms and ideas that were once embraced by one subculture become the terms primarily used by another subculture. Language is important because it guides our conversations and helps shape our ideas and attitudes about social issues.

One of the primary debates regarding the use of language in the fields of disability studies and disability theology revolves around person-first language and identity-first language. While I recognize that the use of language is far more nuanced than a simple binary model might suggest, using the person-first and identity-first designations can help us work through the ideas presented in this book.

Those who prefer person-first language believe that a person is more than their diagnosis; therefore, they should be referred to as a person with a disability. Those who prefer identity-first language believe that disability is central to a person's identity, and therefore it is not necessary to attempt to separate a person from their disability. In other words, identity-first language encourages phrasing such as *an autistic person* rather than *a person with autism*.

It is important to recognize that there are times when neither of these designations quite captures how a person wants to be identified. We must also recognize the need to honor the wishes of those who have a preference. That said, you will find that I will at times use both person-first language and identity-first language in this book and at times will follow the ideals espoused by both positions in order to guide the discussion more clearly.

In the end, the use of the concept and word *disability* will be the primary way that I describe physical, developmental, or intellectual impairment of any variety in this book because it is my belief that as a part of the dismantling of body hierarchy in the church and in society, we must attempt to set aside the idea that the word *disability* is itself the problem. Disability is a natural part of life, and the felt need to use euphemisms to describe human impairment or limitation is often simply a way of trying to avoid a term that society has led us to believe is shameful. Disability is not a dirty word, nor are disabled people less valuable members of our churches and communities, and we should partner with them in dismantling language that suggests otherwise.

ACKNOWLEDGMENTS

The task of putting words to the thoughts and ideas that we grapple with is not easy. Yet somehow, I continue to return to this medium of expressing my ever-evolving faith because, for me, words are transforming. The words that authors use to communicate their ideas convey more than information. Those words are an invitation into a space shaped by a burning desire to be transparent and authentic. In my opinion, there is no greater practice of vulnerability than for one to place their thoughts, questions, and criticisms of the world on a page for others to think about, question, and critique. The life of an author is a life of vulnerability.

The majority of this book was written while I was actively undergoing treatment for stage 3 cancer that developed into stage 4 cancer. To say the least, I was in an extremely vulnerable state, which meant that the support I needed to finish this work was essential to my success. Being able to share my thoughts with the world while battling cancer has turned out to be a wonderful gift that so many supporters helped to make a reality.

To the wonderful people of Tri-Cities Church, I am forever grateful for the countless ways that you provided support and prayers for me during this process. The love, grace, and generosity you shared with my family and me during our most vulnerable time served as the fuel to continue my fight against cancer and my fight to create a better world for disabled people. I consider myself truly blessed to belong to such a wonderful community.

I am also thankful for the scores of people around the world who have been praying for me and supporting me from afar. When I decided to share my cancer journey with the world, I did so because I knew that I would need as many people praying as possible. To those whom I have never met personally yet have prayed for me and supported me, thank you. Your support is proof that despite the many things that can divide us, at our core we are connected, we are family, and we need one another on this journey called life.

Thank you to the team at Brazos Press. Thank you for your support. Thank you for your grace. Thank you for partnering with me in my vision for this work. Thank you for honoring me with a platform on which I can share my work and share my heart. Thank you for providing a space where authors like me can be vulnerable, real, and transparent. Thank you for your guidance along this journey and for making this dream a reality.

Finally, thank you to my family. To my wife, Isabella, thank you for your love and support. Thank you for believing in my work and for pushing me to share myself with the world. Thank you for being willing to share me and my time with the disability community. Thank you for being a partner in advocating for disabled people everywhere. Most of all, thank you for inspiring me to fight cancer with a sense of hopefulness and joy. To my three sons, know that dad loves you and that you are each incredible in your own unique way. Thank you for sharing your dad with the world. Thank you for teaching me how to be more vulnerable and how to both give and receive grace. I love you.

INTRODUCTION

In Their Own Eyes

On September 12, 2001, I had an encounter with police that could have ended far worse than it did. The tension was high that day. Terrorists had attacked our country twenty-four hours earlier. I was a junior manager for a large retail company, and I had just finished up the evening by closing the store. With the night crew inside stocking shelves, I followed protocol by driving my car around the building to be sure that it was secure.

When I reached the side alley of the building, I noticed a car backed in beside an emergency exit door. The car had no license plate. The terrorist attacks weighing heavily on my mind, I was afraid someone may have been hiding in the store. In order to make sure that my night crew was safe, I called the police.

Three to four minutes after calling 911, three or four police cars abruptly surrounded my car. I had no clue what was going on. The drivers were shining their high beams into my car, and the light completely blinded me. I did not know who was there, how many of them were surrounding me, or whether they had guns drawn on me. I froze. Then I cried. I didn't want to die.

Eventually, they yelled through a megaphone to roll my window down and place my hands outside the vehicle. My car didn't have automatic windows, so rolling the window down meant dropping my hands below their line of sight. I couldn't see them, what they were doing, or how close they were to me. I assumed they had their guns drawn, so I stayed frozen. Then I cried more. I didn't dare move a muscle. My fear for my own life told me that as soon as I reached down, they would kill me. So here I was in an alley on the side of a store preparing to meet my Maker because I was certain I was about to be shot.

After what seemed like an eternity, one lone officer approached my car. He must have told his fellow officers to turn off their lights, then he tapped on my window and told me that I was going to be okay, and he kindly asked me again to roll down the window. I was terrified, and he knew it, and he saved me and the other officers from reacting in a way that could have ended my life. I was thankful that he didn't let fear control him or the situation. He did not know me. He did not know that I was the person who made the initial call.

As I reflect on the encounter, two factors played a significant role in the way I reacted: I am Black, and I am autistic. What I wish I had known back then is that many people who are neurodivergent process information differently than those who are neurotypical. Neurodivergence usually includes autism, ADHD, and other neurological differences. One way that neurodivergent brains operate differently has to do with executive functioning, or how the brain absorbs information, organizes it, and acts on the information in a manner that is safe and effective. In intense and high-stress situations, executive functioning can become challenging, if not impossible.

I don't tell this story very often because for so many people these are not unusual occurrences. They happen regularly. I am grateful that those officers spared my life when all the ingredients for a fatal shooting of an unarmed, young Black male were present. I have lived to talk about it, but so many others have not.[1]

Lives Lost

Ahmaud Arbery

I've lived in the Atlanta area for over two decades. Georgia is where I settled after college. It is where I married my wife. It is where our children were born. Georgia is the only place where I have been employed during my adult life. Georgia is home.

With all that the state means to me, I am acutely aware that Georgia is still part of the South, and the South still has more than its fair share of challenges regarding racial bias. On February 23, 2020, at approximately 1:00 p.m., twenty-five-year-old Ahmaud Arbery was shot and killed while jogging in a suburban neighborhood just fifteen minutes outside of downtown Brunswick. The two men who shot him were a father and son, Gregory and Travis McMichael.

Like many people, when I first heard of the murder of Ahmaud, it wasn't on that February day when he lost his life. The distance between where I live and Brunswick isn't so far that I would have missed a news story about a young man being gunned down. The reason I didn't hear what happened to Ahmaud is because it didn't make the news at all, at least not when he was first killed. It wasn't until May, after a cell phone video of the shooting surfaced, that the country found out about this senseless killing.

The local prosecutor had initially declined to indict the two men who shot him. Without the video evidence that clearly shows the McMichaels accosting Ahmaud without provocation, they likely would not have faced criminal charges. Governor Brian Kemp later made this statement about the tragic event: "Ahmaud was a victim of a vigilante style of violence that has no place in Georgia. . . . Some tried to justify the actions of his killers by claiming they had the protection of an antiquated law that is ripe for abuse." Kemp would later sign a hate crime bill after Georgia drew criticism for being one of four states that didn't have a law against such crimes. That law allows judges imposing sentences to increase punishment against those who target victims based on race, color, religion, national origin, sex, sexual orientation, gender, mental disability, or physical disability.[2]

Ahmaud didn't have a weapon, yet his actions to defend himself against two armed strangers were considered aggressive and dangerous enough for law enforcement to accept the McMichaels' account that they acted in self-defense. When the truth came to light, the McMichaels and the man who took the cell phone footage were eventually all found guilty of murder and of committing a hate crime.

Elijah McClain

In August 2019, police in Aurora, Colorado, approached twenty-three-year-old Elijah McClain after they had received a 911 call reporting a "suspicious person" walking down the road in a ski mask and behaving strangely. When officers confronted McClain, he repeatedly asked the officers to let go of him and announced that he was going home. Elijah was a young, Black, autistic man.

Those who have sensory-processing challenges, which are common in autistic individuals, are often averse to touch, especially when they do not initiate contact. The body camera transcripts of the event record McClain repeatedly asking the officers to let him go, pleading with them, "Please respect the boundaries that I am speaking."[3] We can also hear McClain explaining his plan to go home. Another common characteristic of autism is difficulty switching from one activity to the next without a thorough transition or additional time to adjust to the new expectations. The random police officers approaching McClain for an unknown and undisclosed reason most likely interfered with his internalized plan of simply going home.

Finally, we hear Elijah stating, "I'm just different, that's all. I'm just different." Many believe this was Elijah's way of trying to explain his autistic behavior and neurology to officers who deemed his behavior strange and, eventually, dangerous.

Officers at the scene eventually restrained McClain, who weighed only 143 pounds, using a choke hold. When paramedics arrived, an injection of ketamine was administered to calm him down. Because of the strength with which he resisted the officers, they wrongly suspected McClain was on drugs at the time of their encounter. Ketamine is a powerful sedative, and the paramedics administered Elijah a dose that was nearly twice the amount recommended for an individual his size. Shortly thereafter, Elijah stopped breathing. They then took him to the hospital, where he would die three days later.

Elijah McClain had no weapon. His family later reported that Elijah suffered from anemia, which made him cold, so it was not uncommon for him to wear a ski mask in order to keep warm. The investigation found that the Aurora police had no legal basis to stop, frisk, or restrain Elijah.[4] Essentially, Elijah died because of implicit racial and ableist biases.

Implicit racial bias strongly shapes the treatment of people of color in the US judicial system. According to the New York Civil Liberties Union, the NYPD, from 2002 to 2011, conducted stop and frisk procedures on millions of citizens, about 90 percent of those being Black and Hispanic people. Eighty-eight percent of those minorities who the police profiled and stopped had no weapons or contraband.[5] Often, what leads to such practices is the perception that Black and Brown bodies and the behaviors they display are inherently more aggressive—and therefore more dangerous.

There are several research studies that have found that compared to White people, Black people are far more often subject to automatic and subconscious negative stereotypes and prejudice.[6] These thoughts usually extend beyond just negative attitudes; Black and Brown bodies are associated with violence, threatening behavior, and crime. Black men are also more likely to be misremembered for carrying a weapon because of this bias.[7]

Let's be honest: The stories I am sharing with you are not unusual. There's nothing new about the statistics that prove racial bias is a reality in our country. There's nothing new about Black authors, scholars, activists, and clergy speaking up about these issues. What is new, and what I am aiming to bring to this ongoing discussion, is that racial bias in America is not simply an issue of race. It is not simply an issue of skin preference. It is not just an issue of a lack of diversity. Race-based slavery and the enduring racial bias and discrimination it created are about disability discrimination as well. Our issues with racism are in fact issues of ableism—and American Christianity has played a significant role in influencing ableism in our present cultural context.

In Their Own Eyes

There is one underlying factor in all three stories I have shared: interpretation. I define *ableism* as follows:

> *The practice of discriminating against people with disabilities based on the belief that "normal" bodies are superior to those that are not.*

Essentially, it is a hierarchy of bodies. We see ableism, or body hierarchy, working its way silently through the church. Our rites, our rituals, and even our rhetoric often reflect the ways that ableism has infiltrated the faith, especially in Western churches. With a few exceptions, most early Christian traditions stressed the centrality of the body: from the creation account, which explains how human bodies came into being, to the incarnation of God as a human body, even to the numerous New Testament texts that describe the Christian community as a body—namely, the body of Christ. We can even assume the importance of the body when we read of Jesus describing his body as bread and his blood as a cup of wine representing his sacrifice for his followers.

The Christian belief that God became a human speaks volumes about the role of the human body. In fact, it is through the human body that we best understand God's nature, God's character, and God's intentions. In Jesus, God uses the human body to reveal himself. This also means that the way we experience God is through our own bodies. It is impossible to experience God without experiencing him through the bodies we inhabit. This is the beauty of creation. God connects with humanity by using the human body to reveal himself. God comes to me and communicates to me in the disabled Black body that I inhabit. My experience with God is shaped by the way my body works, the way it looks, and the way it is perceived by the culture I live in. Whether you're Black or White, disabled or nondisabled, short or tall, male or female, your body is critically important to how you experience God.

Ableism tends to ignore this reality. It silently pretends that our bodies are unimportant in relation to how we understand and experience God, primarily because people who consider themselves to have normal bodies believe that their experience is the default experience for all bodies. Ableism in religion shows up this way by implicitly assuming that to be disabled or Black or female is a sort of subcategory of humanity that renders the ways those bodies experience God as invalid or unimportant.

Ableism also perpetuates the view that disabled bodies need repair or supervision. It assumes incompetence, regardless of the type or scope of disability. Ableism is the ranking of bodies, but it isn't merely the ranking of which bodies matter most; it is also the ranking of bodies with the intention of holding the power to interpret the behavior and intentions of bodies deemed deficient or disabled. Ableism assumes the power to define which bodies are best and which behaviors are normal or dangerous. This means that Black bodies are often the targets of ableist ideology, an ideology that creates images of normal and ideal bodies that neither Black nor disabled bodies can achieve.

The question is, How does this happen?

Let's first turn to Scripture. The book of Judges includes a line that has always reverberated deep within my soul: "All the people did whatever seemed right in their own eyes" (17:6). This line appears multiple times, which suggests it's important. In a time when there was no king—no communal standard of right and wrong, ethical and unethical, moral and immoral—people created their own path and their own perspective about morality. What's most important about this period in ancient Israel isn't just the idea that moral relativism seemed to be subtly destroying ideas of community; this period produced a certain class of people whose perspectives were prioritized over others.

The story of Micah helps set the stage for answering the question of what has happened:

There was a man named Micah, who lived in the hill country of Ephraim. One day he said to his mother, "I heard you place a curse on the person who stole 1,100 pieces of silver from you. Well, I have the money. I was the one who took it." "The LORD bless you for admitting it," his mother replied. He returned the money to her, and she said, "I now dedicate these silver coins to the LORD. In honor of my son, I will have an image carved and an idol cast." So when he returned the money to his mother, she took 200 silver coins and gave them to a silversmith, who made them into an image and an idol. And these were placed in Micah's house. Micah set up a shrine for the idol, and he made a sacred ephod and some household idols. Then he installed one of his sons as his personal priest. In those days Israel had no king; all the people did whatever seemed right *in their own eyes*. (Judg. 17:1–6, emphasis added)

Of course, you won't find the word *ableism* in the story of Micah. *Ableism* is a fairly new word that helps to define discrimination against disabled people. That said, my use of the story of Micah is about calling ableism what it really is. Ableism is a sin. When we understand ableism as a sin that we often commit, we can then read the story of Micah as a narrative that provides a parallel to how ableism works in religion.

There are three major themes in this story that relate to ableism, racism, and religion. First, there is an initial sin. Micah has stolen a large amount of silver from his mother. While he confesses to his crime, he seems to do so out of fear of the curse. His theft is not something to be taken lightly. Eleven hundred pieces of silver is an extraordinary amount of money. We don't know why he has stolen it. We have no information about how his mother has come to have such a large amount of money. What we do know is that Micah never experiences consequences for his theft. His initial sin goes unaddressed. In the same way, the theft of African bodies that supplied the transatlantic slave trade was an egregious sin of America. Yet the sin that goes unaddressed in history is the sin of ableism, or the ranking of bodies. This is the sin that gives birth to racial bias.

Second, there is the creation of idols and images. Micah's mother uses the silver returned to her to build an image in her son's honor. Rather than holding her son accountable for his sin, she has an image built to honor him. In a similar fashion, American Christianity has often failed to hold the captors of African bodies accountable and has honored those responsible for the sin of slavery and racial discrimination. The erection of monuments and the retelling of history lead to a sense of exceptionalism, or the creation of large egos. Micah's mother makes an exception for his sin. The problem is that excessive exceptions lead to a sense of entitlement. Egos that cast images and create idols serve as the anchor for societal norms.

Images and idols are common in ableist ideology. In order to determine which bodies are best, we create images and place idols in our homes and communities. The challenge in dealing with racial bias is understanding that racism cannot exist without ableism. Disability discrimination is at the heart of racial discrimination because the actual business of slavery is the business of bodies. There are bodies to breed. Bodies to sell. Bodies to work. And bodies to worship. Black Africans were perceived as inherently disabled, which White slaver owners used to justify enslaving them. Just as Micah sets up a shrine in his home to worship the images and idols resulting from his initial sin, so have large swaths of American culture exalted images of "normal" bodies, which have become objects of worship and admiration. The undoing of racism requires the destruction of ableist idols.

Finally, there is the creation of an institution. Following the creation of the image and idol, Micah creates a sacred space in his home and installs his son as his personal priest. The installation of a priest signifies the creation of a religious system, an institution by which Micah organizes his religious life. It is the dawning of a new type of religious experience that is not only centered on created images but also centered on his familial bond with his son. The priest's role is to perform the rites and rituals that are fundamental to worship. The priest facilitates the absolution of sin and one's right standing with God. When Micah appoints his own son as priest, he creates a religious institution in which spiritual leadership requires sameness, in which those who share his likeness are the sole source of spirituality.

In a similar way, we steep American Christianity in the practice of treating sameness as sacred. Bodies that are different aren't invited to lead, and the work that they produce is deemed deficient. Divides about doctrinal issues are just one of the many ways that disability discrimination manifests itself in American Christianity. It's not just about right belief; it's about the right bodies being the only legitimate source for producing right beliefs.

Initial Sin, Idols, and Institutions

Initial sin. Images and idols. Institutions. These are the "big three" of American racial bias, and it all begins with theft.

The transatlantic slave trade was in fact the intentional ranking of bodies. It served as the foundation for deciding which bodies are best, which bodies are most beautiful, how bodies are to behave, where certain bodies belong, and which bodies of work are most credible. Built-in biases are at the core of how Western Christianity was formed and practiced in its earliest stages. This is how ableism has shaped the church and shaped race in America.

People with disabilities live in a world that is not built for them. We have ableist ideology to thank for that. What may not be as obvious, however, is the direct connection between ableism and race and the subsequent ways in which disability and Blackness are intentionally linked. What's also not as obvious is that Western Christianity has been complicit in upholding the sanctity of able-bodiedness.

We attach ableism to Western Christianity like a parasite to a host. In the earliest days of settlement in the Western world, Christianity attached itself to ableist ideology so that it would survive its migration into the new world. Ableism fed the practice of Christianity in the West; not only did it help aid the church's survival, but it also helped it to grow and to become a powerful force in influencing how society has viewed minority bodies, both Black and disabled. Ableism is America's initial sin, and much like the story of Micah in the book of Judges, American Christianity has built images, idols, and a massive institution all fueled by ableism, and it did so without ever having to make amends for its initial sin: the buying and selling of African bodies.

While my aim is to be objective, I know keenly that my personal experience with disability, race, and religion will shape this project. After years of struggling with a host of issues, such as social anxiety and sensory processing challenges—none of which I had the language to explain so that I could better understand and be understood—I was diagnosed with autism in December 2014. I was thirty-six and married with three children. I had a professional career as a pastor, had a master's degree, and was working on my first doctoral degree. From the outside looking in, my life was very successful, yet there were invisible struggles that had a profound impact on my relationships and my employment.

As early as the age of seven or eight years old, I noticed some significant differences between me and other children my age. I often found it difficult to relate socially with my peers. The world seemed to have an inside joke that I wasn't in on. This would eventually turn into a lifetime of relational and social struggles that affected my life significantly.

My life as an American, pastor, author, scholar, husband, and father is lived out at the intersection of disability, race, and religion. I am intimately and eternally tied to this reality, and I feel compelled to write about it because I am convinced that the path to ridding our culture of racism is to name ableism and discrimination against bodies deemed deficient as the root cause of racial bias and racial injustice. Ableism fuels bias, and this book is a challenge to the sin of ableism and a call to the church to act justly. This book is about searching for the truth while centering the voices of the disability community and the Black community in the much-needed, long-overdue conversation about the role that Christianity has played in the struggle for inclusion and justice in America.

I confess this book almost did not become a reality. Truth be told, I tried with every fiber of my being to avoid writing it because I knew what I would have to say, whom I would have to say it to, and what the cost would be for saying what I am going to say. I wanted to write a different book. Then, one day, I heard a friend say during a podcast interview that if you set out to write something that will be popular, you will rarely end up with a work that is prophetic. His words pierced my soul to the core and reminded me that, as a follower of Jesus, I am accountable for sharing the truth. For Black bodies, disabled bodies, and Black and disabled bodies, both Western culture and Western Christianity have historically been enemies to progress. Ableist ideology creates the world in its own image and in its own eyes.

This book is my public acceptance of my call to trade in popularity for a chance to walk in the prophetic tradition of Jesus. What comes next will be challenging, and my prayer is that you commit to taking this journey with me.

This book will address what I am calling the "big three" of bias. Throughout the book I will explore the initial sin of American culture and American Christianity. In order to do this, we will take a trip back in time to the early 1600s, with an examination of Puritan theology in American culture and how it introduced, intertwined, and ultimately influenced views on both disability and race. I will go on to examine American Christianity's construction of images and idols, including the manufacturing of an image of Jesus that distances him from his own humanity, from disability, and from human limitation. Then I will argue how the church as an institution has produced congregations that idolize sameness, repudiate disability, and enable racism and racial bias in our culture. The phrase "in their own eyes" doesn't just represent a period in Israel's history known as the time of the judges; it also represents the way in which America has historically been structured by a singular story, a singular perspective about what and who is right. The phrase is about our human tendency to use difference to create power dynamics. Ableism and racism are declarations of difference, and declaring others as different means they are different from someone else. But who decides what differences are desirable or undesirable?

I hope this book will challenge everything you believe about disability, race, and religion in American culture. My prayer is that I do my job well enough that it challenges you to rethink how the church in America can use its massive influence to address issues of ableism within its walls, within its theology, within its rhetoric, and within our culture so that we can eradicate disability and racial discrimination. Addressing ableism is hard work, but I am convinced that this hard work is worth doing because Jesus has made a promise and a prediction. He has promised that he would build his church and that the church would outlast even the greatest attempts to defeat its purpose.

On the day of his first sermon in his hometown, Jesus opens the scroll of Isaiah the prophet and reads the words that make this work worthwhile. "The Spirit of the LORD is upon me, for he has anointed me to bring Good News to the poor. He has sent me to proclaim that captives will be released, that the blind will see, that the oppressed will be set free, and that the time of the LORD's favor has come" (Luke 4:18–19). The same Spirit that lays claim to Jesus is laying claim to his church to bring good news, freedom, healing, and hope to the world because the day of God's justice is here, and God is choosing us as partners.

Disability, Blackness, and Early American Christianity

They Say / We Say

There's a saying that if you've met one person with autism, then you've met one person with autism. Autism is truly a spectrum, not because we should view it as some linear scale that ranges from zero to ten or from not very autistic to extremely autistic. Autism is far too complex to simplify it in those terms. Instead, we should see autism as more like a color wheel in which, depending on factors such as environment, age, gender, and sociological circumstances, the common traits associated with autism are sometimes more pronounced in certain areas than in others. All the traits are there, but they may not be experienced equally by those who are observing.

Some common identifiers exist among all autistic people. So at the risk of overgeneralizing, I want to focus on an aspect of autism that is most true about everyone diagnosed with it. Many autistic people have a deeply held special interest, usually in a topic or subject that appeals to them. Special interests can change over the years, and most people only pay attention to this aspect of autism when they see it in children. However, autistic adults also have special interests, and many of them, such as myself, have connected their special interest to their vocational journey.

When I was a child, I loved to read. Reading was the way I made sense of the world, especially because I didn't really understand people. Like many young children, I enjoyed reading fiction, but nonfiction especially captured my attention. There was something compelling about reading stories that were true. In fact, my special interest as a child was absorbing as much history as I could. I loved history. History tells the story of "how." How things are made. How people became famous. How we arrived where we are now. As a child, I can vividly remember being so enthralled with history that I would sit and read through the encyclopedia volumes my parents ordered from door-to-door salespeople. (I guess I'm really showing my age here.) I loved researching a variety of time periods. I loved learning the history associated with the geography lessons we were studying in school. As a military brat, I even recall taking special school field trips while living in Germany to learn about some of the medieval history connected to the region. I was in heaven. History captured my young, autistic heart and mind. To this day, I love watching documentaries and reading biographies and studying first-century church history. In my world, history is central. It is what shapes my life in profoundly spiritual ways. It helps me understand what is happening around me and what is happening to me.

History is important, and as you'll see in this chapter, it is important to understand the extremely complicated intersection between ableism, racism, and the practice of Christianity in the West. While I am not a historian by profession, I know the need for an accurate portrayal of the stories that shape society and culture. In American culture, the practice of storytelling has rightfully come under suspicion because as a nation we are increasingly realizing that many stories about race, disability, class, and gender have been almost entirely omitted from the story of our founding.

I believe we are in a battle for history, not because we don't have access to what happened but because we have significantly downplayed the impact that the omission of those stories has had on shaping current views and norms in our country and in our churches. In addition to the challenge of reclaiming the stories of minorities and the disabled that have been omitted from our nation's history, there needs to be an admission that the supposed deficiency of Black and disabled bodies is still present. This residue can often be seen in the practices and policies that shape both our country and our churches. But history can only truly be history if in fact those elements of our society are truly in the past.

Simply put, it is not history if it is still happening. We are stuck in the limited historical narrative of the West. We seldom stop to acknowledge or embrace the complete story of the American experiment. Until we do so, we will continue to allow the parts of the past that we selectively choose to highlight to shape our present reality.

This is why it's important to dedicate a chapter to understanding ableism, racism, and Western Christianity. This historical journey will be information to some and complete revelation to others, but what I want more than anything else is for the journey to be seen not as an exhaustive history of ableism and racism in America but as a survey of the important events in our nation's founding that still very much impact how we view the world we inhabit. Here I call attention to the not-so-rose-colored glasses that we have all been peering through, mostly unaware of the impact that tint has on influencing our ideas about disability and race.

Ableism and Antebellum America

European colonization has, from its inception, always been heavily shaped by ideas about ability and disability. Even before the first ships arrived on the shores of the new world, beliefs about which bodies were most "desirable" influenced decisions about those deemed worthy enough to make the trip across the Atlantic. Able-bodiedness was a prerequisite to prosperity in the new world. As a result, colonialism designed nearly every American system with the intention of exploiting or erasing disability. Enslaved Africans were most affected by this ideology, and it would carry them across the Atlantic in chains to fulfill the European dream of acquiring wealth and power.

Federal law defines *disability* as "a physical or mental impairment that substantially limits one or more major life activities of [an] individual; a record of such an impairment; or being regarded as having such an impairment."[1] This definition is important for two reasons. First, we define disability as an impairment that limits engagement in major life activities. By this definition, disability is viewed as not meeting social expectations and social demands. We cannot define disability apart from a social construct of perceived normal abilities. Second, disability requires a person to be regarded as disabled. This means that a social construct primarily decides what makes someone disabled. This privileges and prefers able-bodiedness by using certain types of bodies as the standard for what types of minds and bodies not only are acceptable but are necessary for production and success.

Historically, the Western world has long been guided by societal definitions of disability. Disability historian Kim Nielsen writes:

> From the very beginning of the European colonization of North America, before the ships making the ocean passage even left European ports, disability and definitions of bodies and minds shaped the experience. Those directing the long voyages across the Atlantic excluded individuals with bodies and minds deemed undesirable or unlikely to survive the voyage, which could be arduous, even for the most robust. Adventurers, wealth seekers, and colonists who died during the treacherous and unpleasant journey were thrown overboard. The determination of "able-bodied" depended on the perception that one conformed to communal expectations regarding class, gender, and religion.[2]

Among all the communal expectations and norms that shaped definitions of disability during early Western settlement, none had a greater influence than the role of religion. In 1620, English Puritans settled in Massachusetts. These settlers made their home in a region now known as Plymouth, Massachusetts, and are most famously known and remembered as the pilgrims who were among the first to settle in America.

The Puritans brought a social ethic that informed their ideal social order, which shaped how they sought to create a thriving community. They were convinced that creation had a natural order designed by God, and they wanted to reproduce that order in their communities. Their religious convictions were closely aligned with the way they settled in New England as family units, in distinction from the way the English settled as individuals in the Chesapeake Bay area. While both groups had ideals about the bodies that were best suited for their goals, the Puritans of Plymouth attached their hopes and aspirations to definitions of able-bodiedness that were closely aligned with their ideas of family.

Prior to settling in the new land, women, according to Puritan religious convictions, were considered a subordinate class to men. Although that structure remained in place, Plymouth Puritan leaders set family as an ideal goal for colonization in New England; therefore, women who could bear children were deemed appropriately able-bodied. As a result, they linked the earliest definitions of ability and disability to religious and social ideals of family and economic prosperity through farming.

The Dawn of "Disability"

As early as 1636, definitions of disability shaped the Puritan social order of family and farming. Initially, settlers established that the colony would help maintain the standard of living for any male citizen who became unable to work because of a disabling injury that occurred during active duty in the military. In 1641, however, a more robust policy surfaced that gave a more definitive understanding of how the Puritans' religious convictions shaped their ideas of disability. The Massachusetts "Body of Liberties" provided protection for the disabled by asserting that people who were too young or too old, or who had mental or physical limitations, would not be held to community performance standards. This statute also provided "protection" from making unsound financial decisions, and it included the young, the elderly, and even women in its description of those deemed as unfit to have a say in matters of commerce.

The Puritan ethic centered on male led families, structured to bring economic prosperity to the colony. That meant defining the bodies and minds that best fit this new social structure in a way that reflected Puritan religious beliefs. To maintain an orderly and religiously responsible community, disability was defined in terms of assets and liabilities. While a significant component of that definition is economically motivated, there was a very critical exception to the definition that highlights the reality that religion shaped early definitions of disability more than anything else. That exception was what was called "monstrous births."

There was little tolerance or accommodation for children born with physical disabilities, especially when the child had an unsightly physical abnormality. Europeans believed that deformities in newborn infants resulted from the mother's lifestyle choices. They believed monstrous births were caused by a range of deviant behaviors, from ungodly thoughts to sexual deviance by the mother.

Puritan theology emphasized order, and in that order was the concept of a deity that showed his displeasure with a deviant woman by inflicting on her and the entire family a child whose physical features fell outside the realm of what was "normal." Women who conducted their lives according to the divine order of the family and of the colony would find themselves as one of God's chosen. Those who did not were punished with disabled children. History records perhaps the most extreme application of this theology when both Anne Hutchinson (1591–1643) and Mary Dyer (1611–60) were charged with having produced monstrous births because of their disobedience to the Puritan religious and social order. In 1637, Hutchinson was charged with heresy on account of having hosted several theological discussions in her own home—as a woman, she was believed unsuited to lead in such a capacity. Hutchinson and everyone who attended her discussion, including Dyer, were tried for subverting the religious, social, and political order as prescribed by Puritan theology.

During this trial, the most pervasive piece of evidence used to prove Hutchinson's and Dyer's guilt was monstrous birth. In 1637, Dyer experienced a stillbirth, and in 1638, Hutchinson also had what governor John Winthrop (1588–1649) described as a monstrous birth. After the heresy trial, Hutchinson, along with her family and her followers, was exiled to Rhode Island. Eventually, in 1660, Dyer was hanged in Boston as a Quaker dissident. She was the first European woman to be hanged in the colonial period.

The rhetoric born out of early Puritan theology also served as the foundation for the creation of racial slavery. In 1619, the first Africans arrived on the shores of North America; by the mid-1600s, racial slavery was embedded in the colonial social, economic, and legal framework. As early as 1640, disability weaved its way into the narrative of the newly forming nation. Racial slavery in the West began by using disability to make chattel slavery a matter of charity rather than a matter of equality. Defining Africans as mentally inferior and effectively disabled allowed for proslavery advocates to appeal to the Christian ethos of benevolence.

One example of how religious language was used to shape ideas about disability is the release of George Fitzhugh's now infamous defense of slavery, *Cannibals All! or Slaves without Masters*. Fitzhugh argues there that slavery is in fact humane when considered against the free labor system of the North. Fitzhugh paved the way for developing the use of disability to define Blackness and to further raise political and social support for racial slavery.

Fitzhugh's work helped popularize the "positive good" argument. Proslavery thought has a long and complicated trajectory in the United States, and we can see this in its attempts throughout history to use religious rhetoric and economic and political arguments for the necessity of slavery. In the decade prior to the Civil War (1861–65), national proslavery arguments absorbed the ideology of the proslavery arguments emerging from the South. As the 1830s ended, the positive good thesis grew in popularity thanks to Senator John C. Calhoun (1782–1850), who preached the message that racial slavery was an act of benevolence. His arguments drew on existing religious, economic, and political arguments, and he expanded them to create a view of racial slavery that centered its practice on the kindness and charity of the slaveholder.

Calhoun's argument marked the beginning stage of using disability imagery to obligate the slaveholder with a duty to exercise authority over enslaved Africans, who ostensibly couldn't care for themselves because of disability, in the same way that they exercised authority in their households. Some twenty years later, Calhoun's speech and use of disability imagery and rhetoric would serve as the foundation for Fitzhugh's less nuanced version of the positive good argument. For Fitzhugh, the positive good argument would evolve from viewing slavery as simply an act of charity by the slaveholder to using disability imagery to assert a sense of the enslaved being extremely content, even happy, with their status as slaves.

Like Calhoun's argument, Fitzhugh's had an ableist undercurrent. It used disability to argue for the ethical view of racial slavery in the United States. In doing so, it created a rationale that connected able-bodiedness to labor and implied that the enslaved were content because, despite their disability, they were cared for by their slaveholders. Using disability imagery as something undesirable became central to the rhetoric of the positive good ideology because it centralized charity, pity, shame, and even distrust of abolitionists as ethical, moral, and religious issues obliging the nation to embrace slavery, not merely as an institution but as a conviction driven by a sense of religious duty.

Of course, religion deeply shaped antislavery arguments and the abolitionist movement. Abolitionist thought was influenced by the Second Great Awakening (ca. 1795–ca.

1835) and the revivalism that spanned the eighteenth century and lasted until the mid-1840s. A Christian ethos of benevolence and charity also guided abolitionists. Unfortunately, those views also produced perspectives about disability that were sometimes *more* damaging than the religious views that motivated proponents of racial slavery. Abolitionists thought people with disabilities were suffering because they were trapped inside defective bodies.

Abolitionists perpetuated the notion that slaves needed guidance because they did not have the capacity to determine their own best interests. In this way, abolitionists also linked Blackness to disability in harmful ways. Abolitionist rhetoric depicted slaves as dependent because of disability and therefore unable to benefit from their own labor. In addition, many abolitionists used disability language to rouse White sympathy by framing disability as a problem that could be fixed with formal education. This further stigmatized Black people as intellectually inferior.

The abolitionist movement used disability imagery to describe the impact that the institution of slavery had on the nation. Adherents often described the institution of slavery as "monstrous," a term closely associated with descriptions of the disabled. They also described individual proponents of racial slavery as "frantic" or "insane," terms otherwise used to describe persons with intellectual disabilities.

An important document of this time is from Henry Parker. Born in 1835, he was a slave of Benjamin Cooper until the age of twenty-four. In 1859, Parker, along with his mother and two sisters, crossed the Ohio River and followed the Underground Railroad to freedom. Parker writes about his experience in a short autobiography. Parker and many other enslaved Black people wrote about their experiences in a genre now known as fugitive slave narratives.

Fugitive slave narratives describe the horrific conditions that enslaved Black people endured because of racial slavery. Testimonies from White antislavery advocates often lent credibility to the first-person eyewitness accounts of former slaves. Fugitive slave narratives played an important part in raising the sympathies of abolitionists, and they often relied heavily on principles of Christian charity and benevolence. Parker's autobiography includes this motif. Three central ideas frame his brief biography. He writes heavily about his faith, descriptively about his family, and about the disabling nature of enslavement in America.

In his narrative, Parker says he is blind. He writes candidly about what led to his loss of vision. Parker combines the story of his enslavement with details about the onset of his disability. His book seeks to arouse the compassion and sympathy of his readers, especially since he encourages readers to purchase the book in order to receive his prayers, the prayers of a blind man. The autobiography of Henry Parker is an important document in helping shape an understanding of the impact of disability and ableism and their intersection with religious rhetoric, rites, and rituals, as well as how all this informs our understanding of disability in American society and culture.

Civil Rights and the Americans with Disabilities Act

Although I'm skipping ahead by more than a century, it's important to note that religion continues to shape how disability is viewed in the modern era. As one example, let's look at the ways religious groups have lobbied to be exempt from the Americans with Disabilities Act (ADA) since 1990.

In the United States, until the ADA, people with disabilities had little recourse to address discrimination. Before then, it was perfectly legal for restaurants to refuse service to disabled people. Employers could refuse to hire a person with a disability solely based on disability. It was also legal to lack necessary accommodations, such as wheelchair ramps, elevators, and accessible bathroom stalls in buildings.

The disability rights movement is considered an offshoot of the civil rights movement. Similar to the Civil Rights Act (CRA) of 1964, the ADA was established to place federal mandates in motion that prevent discrimination against disabled people because of their disability. The law covers a range of physical, developmental, and intellectual disabilities and includes legal consequences for employers who discriminate against disabled applicants or current employees. It also includes legal recourse when buildings such as restaurants, schools, grocery stores, and hotels fail to provide access to those with physical disabilities. The ADA allows for the use of service animals in public spaces.

In 1990, disability activists staged what is now known as the "Capitol Crawl." Scores of disabled people pulled themselves up the one hundred steps of the capitol building to highlight the lack of accessibility. The intent was to create a far-reaching and long-lasting image that would liberate the disability community. The Capitol Crawl, like many of the events of the civil rights movement, turned the activism of marginalized people into a striking and unsettling icon, a symbol of the lack of liberty available to those with disabilities.

Civil rights and disability rights intersect in the search for liberty. In 1962, John F. Kennedy signed the Mental Health and Mental Retardation Reform Act.[3] Kennedy was concerned with the custodial isolation of persons with intellectual disabilities, and he said it was a fundamental obstruction of liberty. H. Rutherford Turnbull III is an author, educator, and scholar in the area of disability policy and law. He notes that "in Kennedy's view, custodial isolation is the antithesis of liberty, especially when the isolation is compelled. Community concern and capability are the antidotes to isolation and the vehicles to liberty."[4] Judges serving on Kennedy's task force described the dilemma by stating that "liberty is a freedom of choice within the general system of laws and social values. The individual's liberty is impaired when he is not permitted the same range of choices as his peers."[5]

Like Kennedy, Martin Luther King Jr. also heralded the call to liberty, a liberty that was best described as a freedom to choose. In June of 1966, King used his powerful oratory skills to call the nation to account for its failure to progress toward desegregation in the South. King's sermon titled "Guidelines to a Constructive Church" opened with him explaining that twelve years after *Brown v. Board of Education*, in which the Supreme Court ruled that segregation in public education was unconstitutional, desegregation in the South had only amounted to 1 percent integration.[6] The incredibly slow implementation of this ruling was seen not just as an obstruction of choice but also as the restriction of liberty for Black bodies. In the case of both Kennedy and King, the anecdote to old narratives about disability and Blackness was liberty—in other words, an unrestricted story of what it means to be human, to be healthy, and to be a valued citizen in America.

The ADA resulted from the disability community being inspired and challenged by the civil rights movement and the passing of the CRA, which was a landmark piece of federal legislation that made it illegal to discriminate based on race, color, religion, sex, or national origin. The legislation would later add sexual orientation and gender identity as additional forms of discrimination that would be outlawed.

The CRA, led largely by the historically Black church, was anchored in equality and equity. Because of its close connection to the Black church, there was also an element of spirituality that guided the cause. The spirituality of the Black church was often in conflict with the practice of the Christian religion in the colonial United States because it contested the version of Christianity that led to racial slavery and discrimination. That said, it was the church that led the push to pass the CRA. In contrast, the disability rights movement and the subsequent passing of the ADA had far less of a connection to the faith community. If the ADA was modeled after the CRA, then why did the faith community have little to no role in the pursuit of equality for the disability community? What led the church to distance itself from advocating for a marginalized community as it once did in the civil rights movement? The answer is found in a landmark case about disability rights that eventually turned into a case about religious liberty.

Disability Rights and Religious Liberty

In 1974, Larry and Sandi Zobrest gave birth to their first child, Jim, while living in Erie, Pennsylvania. Jim was diagnosed as profoundly deaf after a routine medical examination before his first birthday. Jim would later attend a private preschool for children with disabilities; however, after learning that he would be sent to a public school system that lacked accommodations for his disability, the family moved to Tucson, Arizona, where Jim would attend the state-operated Arizona School for the Deaf and Blind. There, he received a taxpayer-funded sign language interpreter. After several years of struggling with Jim's education, the Zobrests moved away from Tucson and returned to Erie, eventually enrolling Jim in a Roman Catholic school.

When Jim was enrolled in this private school, however, the district it was a part of denied him the use of an interpreter, citing that it would be unlawful to use state funds at a religious school. The Zobrest family sued the school district. They were under the impression that state funds could be used to provide their son with assistance at a private Catholic school. In their view, denying their son the assistance he needed was due to their religious choices. While the federal government allows for religious liberty, using federal funds to support their child at a private religious institution seemed to violate the law that prohibits the federal government from preferring one religion over another. The case introduced a tension between religion and disability rights in American discourse.

The contest over who would pay for Jim's interpreter went on for six years, five of which were in court. During that time, Jim graduated from high school. Eventually, the focus on disability rights took a back seat to the focus on religious freedom in education. This happened because both parties involved in the lawsuit decided to frame the case in terms of religious freedom rather than disability law.

The Zobrest family eventually received a favorable decision from the US Supreme Court. There was renewed hope that the landmark case would provide relief for the disabled. But in reality, in order for the Zobrests to win, religious liberty had to take precedence over disability rights. This is partly why, in 1990, upon the passing of the ADA, religious institutions could exempt themselves from the requirements of the ADA on the grounds of religious liberty.

The bigger issue, one that often goes unnoticed, is that with the use of religious liberty as a means of exempting themselves from providing federally mandated accommodations for disabled people, religious institutions also effectively distanced themselves from practicing a faith that demands involvement in social justice. If you have ever wondered why there is so much tension in the modern church involving social justice, it is because as soon as the church was able to use religious liberty to opt out of creating a more just world for the disabled, it became easier to continue to fracture the connection between faith and justice. The exemption of the church from the ADA based on religious liberty has had a far greater impact than just providing accommodations for disabled people; it also became the platform for many churches and congregations to distance themselves from practicing racial justice.

The Road to Racism

Ableism, Religion, and Racial Bias

In 2020, when I was diagnosed with stage 3 colorectal cancer, I had just had my annual physical. I was attending CrossFit classes three to five times a week and had transitioned to a plant-based diet. My book *Disability and the Church* was going to be released in early 2021. I was finally managing to get the hang of leading a church through a global pandemic. I was just beginning to regain my sense of hope and clarity after months of meandering through the misery of COVID-19. Then suddenly, without warning, amid what was feeling like a pretty good life during a pretty challenging year, I learned I had cancer. I felt like life was sending me mixed messages.

Perhaps you recall playing the game of telephone as a child. When my classmates and I played it at my elementary school, our teacher would have us form a circle. Once all of us were in a circle, the teacher would whisper a sentence or phrase into the first student's ear. The rules of the game were simple. The speaker could only share the phrase once and the listener could not ask questions. The listener then would turn to the next student in the circle and repeat the phrase to the best of their ability. This process would repeat until the last student received the message and repeated it out loud, usually resulting in a huge laugh because the message had transformed to the point of making little to no sense at all. The teacher would then share what the original message was so that the class could see just how much the message had changed.

I vividly remember this game because it was the very illustration my oncologist used when he sat down with my wife and me to explain what was happening in my body. He explained that cancer cells are cells that grow without maintaining the original genetic message. As a result, the mixed messages create something unhealthy.

I also think of the telephone game when it comes to describing the history of race, racism, slavery, and segregation in America. The story of race in America is riddled with mixed messages and missing words. Among those words that are missing is *ableism*.

Many people point to race-based slavery as the underlying cause of enduring racism in America. This is true. The legacy of race-based slavery in America continues to plague the country with unresolved and complicated issues because of the subjugation of Black bodies. I am not here to argue against the sinfulness or the ravenous nature of race-based biases, which have entangled themselves into the fabric of the American experiment. Racism is real and is a genuine problem. Still, when it comes to understanding the development of race-based bias, the story is incomplete.

Even prior to the transatlantic slave trade, we see early developments of an ableist system that ranked the value of the bodies brought to the new land. In one of the oldest historical references to Africans in North America, a settler named John Rolfe (ca. 1585–1622) referenced some twenty Africans as merchandise. It had not yet been determined if these Africans were indentured servants or if they were doomed to a lifetime of slavery; however, it is apparent that these Africans held a lower status than their White Virginian counterparts. This serves as evidence that even before racial slavery became the primary reason why Africans were brought to the West, their bodies were ranked as inherently inferior to White bodies. It appears that ableism was at work early in the development of American culture. This perception of inferiority based on race is at the heart of my argument that Black bodies were categorized as disabled bodies.

Before the explosion of the slave trade, the presence of Africans in North America prompted the need for constructing a social order that ensured that, based on their difference, they would never access the prosperity of the New World. So a caste system was created. The separation of Black bodies from White settlers in the workforce was the foundation for a social, political, economic, and spiritual caste system that would make the soon-coming slave trade a possibility.

Ableism, racism, and religion combined to contribute to a Westernized caste system. Religion (i.e., Christianity), not race, was actually the first delineating factor that colonists used to create a caste system that would insulate themselves from the low social status they had experienced in Europe. One of the first ways we see this applied is in the colonists' relationship with the Indigenous people of the land.

In her best-selling book, *Caste: The Origins of Our Discontents,* Isabel Wilkerson explains that the first census conducted in the colony showed a move toward a caste system. She notes that though there were Africans in the colony, they were not listed in the census by name. Europeans who lived in the colony, even those who were indentured servants, were full members of the colony. They were registered in the census by name, age, and date of arrival in the New World. Well before an official union of the states, Africans were not considered equal to their European counterparts.

Any student of American history is aware of this. Even if you did not know about the developments of the American caste system, you could certainly examine documents from the seventeenth and eighteenth centuries and determine that Western society was intentionally divided into distinct categories for creating a subordinate class. What fewer people know is that race was *not* the first tool used to define social status in the colonies. According to Wilkerson, "At first, *religion* . . . defined the status of people in the colonies. Christianity, as a proxy for Europeans, exempted European workers from lifetime enslavement."[1]

Returning to the story of Micah that we explored in chapter 1, we see how Micah uses religion as a mechanism for exemption. This is what he does to avoid being cursed. Even though his mother has placed a curse on the person who stole her money, once Micah confesses, we never see her follow through with her curse. It's not a stretch to consider that nepotism, or kinship-based favoritism, plays a role in her response. (We will eventually discuss the role of spiritual nepotism in creating religious imagery and symbolism that favors certain body types.) Micah successfully uses religious confession to exempt himself from any suffering associated with his initial sin.

Micah's initial sin is a staggering representation of the heart of human sin and the heart of colonization. This sin is to take what belongs to others while simultaneously seeking to exempt ourselves from all consequences. The most effective way to accomplish this goal is to lean on religion and religious rhetoric, religious rites and rituals, and religious ideas of redemption. An example of this is the initial sin of taking land and resources from Indigenous people in American history. Christianity was always the main support of European colonization. By converting Indigenous people to Christianity, Europeans believed they could conform them to European ideals and standards without having to extend to them the rights and privileges they reserved for themselves.

The colonial agenda meant assimilating Indigenous peoples into European culture, a culture that included ideals, religious practices, and social norms that were not germane to Indigenous people. Marriage was used to assimilate Indigenous people into a Christian and European identity. European men sought to marry Indigenous women, convert them to Christianity, give them proper English names, and father children who could then escape what colonialists believed to be hereditary heathenism. This strategy, however, was not nearly as successful as they anticipated, because Indigenous women quickly learned that becoming Christian meant becoming European and abandoning their tribal and cultural identity.

Here's where the story of race in America morphs into something that doesn't mirror its origins. Like rogue cancer cells, the messages about race and racial bias in American history have slowly transformed into a history that is both unhealthy and unhelpful in trying to bring course correction to a troubled social system. Rather than start with race as the original delineating factor that props up the American caste system, we have to take a sobering look at the role that Christianity played in developing a caste system in colonial America.

In the beginning, Christianity served as a successful status symbol in the colonies. Colonial efforts relied heavily on religion as the primary tool for asserting one's superior nature, intellect, and spirituality. To be Christian was to be superior, and to be Christian meant one would essentially be exempt from suffering. After all, the colonies had been established primarily to escape British rule and to ascend to a more privileged class, a class that most people never enjoyed under British rule. In the beginning, to be Christian meant to be European, which also meant that early settlers believed that their religious identity provided them with the moral standing to place themselves at the top of the caste system.

Europeans saw the peoples of the new land as uneducated, uncultured, unchristian, and, because of their spiritual practices and skin color, inferior. This became especially true when their efforts to smother tribal and cultural

identity through marriage were unsuccessful. Religion—
Christianity in particular—became the vehicle for discrimination. As such, the Christian religion did not migrate into
the West simply because of missionaries seeking to share
their faith with Indigenous peoples. Rather, Christianity's
primary purpose in migrating to the West was to mitigate
suffering and servitude for White Europeans.

Eventually, Europeans used the Christian religion as a
tool to construct their caste system that relegated the millions of Africans being imported to the New World to the
lowest tier. Perhaps Christianity could indoctrinate and
civilize the mentally, emotionally, and spiritually inferior
African peoples who were brought to the colonies to build
the nation. It is important to note that Europeans did not
introduce the Christian religion to Africans. There is historical evidence that Christianity had spread to various
parts of the continent of Africa long before the transatlantic slave trade. Christianity had likely long migrated into
Africa through Egypt, Ethiopia, and North Africa, and it
was migrating throughout the continent at the time. African
people had their own rich history of practicing several traditional and tribal religions, as well as Islam. Despite what
European settlers and historians have asserted, people of
African descent were not heathens who lacked religious
devotion.

Yet still, the Christian faith was used as a tool for creating converts who would eternally remain subservient to
European culture. When enslaved Africans began embracing Christianity, Europeans realized that religion could no
longer be the singular delineating marker between them
and those in the lower caste. The shift from religious-based

bias to race-based bias kept White Europeans at the top of the social, political, and economic ladder. For example, missionaries who evangelized and baptized Africans made sure that enslaved Africans knew that conversion in no way implied equality with Whites and that entrance into the faith did not recuse them from obeying their owners. The Christianity handed to enslaved Africans had zero focus on the day-to-day material conditions of Black bodies in the colonies. The baptism of Africans into the Christian faith by European missionaries was often accompanied by vows that slaves had to recite, acknowledging that they knew that their salvation only impacted the condition of their souls and not the material conditions they endured.

The problem, of course, is that this faith does not mirror the faith in the God of Israel. The God of Israel we encounter in Scripture is a God of justice. Despite the fact that the Bible portrays the God of Israel as the God of justice—the God who sides with the marginalized and the oppressed—the Western version of Christianity developed by determining that the gospel of Jesus and the God of justice had no power to bring liberation to slaves in America. This was an intentional move by colonialists.

In making Black bodies exempt from the complete impact of the gospel, we see the evil of ableism operating within Western Christianity. By adjusting the faith to meet the economic goals of slavery, the colonists effectively changed the Jesus narrative into one of their greatest tools to perpetuate injustice and inequality—except this time religion provided the discipline needed to separate the caste system by body types and not just belief. Black bodies were inherently inferior, at least according to colonial-era Christianity, and it is here that we see the religious use of ableism in propping up racial bias in America.

The Christian faith arrived in the West as a means to an end. The reason it came, the route it took, and the associated residual effects all highlight that the Christian faith served the colonial agenda and White European colonists. The story of Jesus migrated to the Western world in the same capacity as an enslaved African did: as an indentured servant to White European colonists. From the outset, Christianity was hijacked as a resource for creating castes more so than a religion that liberated marginalized people.

In fact, the faith itself was not free. It, too, was a slave sent to serve the masters who brought the religion across the waters of the Atlantic. These masters shackled Christianity to a system of oppression from the beginning, failing to live out their faith in a way that was consonant with the teachings of the New Testament. The problem—one often not discussed, as it relates to religion and race—is that while enslaved Africans were eventually freed from their servitude to White America, the faith remained in chains. The people are now free, but the faith is not. So ableism and racism and all other forms of marginalization remain entangled in our practice of Christianity today. We have yet to free the Christian faith from its service to the colonial agenda. We need another emancipation proclamation—this time, one that will free the story of Jesus, the God of justice, and the power of the gospel from the chains of ableism.

John Piper and the Politics
of Desirability

A Letter from My Wife on the First Anniversary of My Autism Diagnosis

One of the greatest myths about autism is that autistic people lack emotion and empathy. Growing up, I wasn't the best at making friends, but I somehow seemed to develop meaningful relationships along the way. When I was eighteen years old, I met someone who would change my life forever. Ours is a story that defies the myths that autism and love cannot coexist. Much later, in December 2014, a therapist would officially diagnose me with autism. December is my "autism anniversary," and on the first year following my diagnosis, my wife, Isabella, wrote the following letter to me, which was eventually shared publicly on my website.

Dear Lamar,

I am writing you this letter almost a year from the time that you were first diagnosed with autism spectrum disorder. I just wanted to let you know how extremely proud I am of you as your wife. First, because you were brave enough to recognize you needed to get evaluated and seek a professional diagnosis when you knew certain things weren't quite adding up. So many are yet to take that step, so I really applaud you!

Second, I am inspired by how much work you're doing to learn about yourself. I heard you say in the interview with Autism Live that you have to learn who you are again at the age of 37. I can't even imagine what that must be like. I applaud you for just having the courage to take that big step and embrace who you are—"fearfully and wonderfully made"—and being OK with who God created you to be and using all your God-given gifts and talents to learn more about the world you have become a part of.

Your response is going to help fill some big gaps, and you're already becoming such a huge voice for a platform that is oftentimes forgotten about and never ever talked about. I see all the work you're doing and how committed you are to autism spectrum disorder issues. Your work in the autism world is going to make huge footprints and lead the way for so many who are already a part of it or will become a part of it.

One thing I realized once we started this journey is that I am having to learn who you are all over again. I have known you for 18-plus years, and we will have been married for 15 years in January next year. While your diagnosis does mean having to learn a new you, I am still googly-eyed over you!

Some would question me and say, "Wow, aren't you concerned this isn't the same man who you married?" And I would say, "No, this is exactly the man I married. We have just arrived at a point in our life where layers are being peeled off and growth is taking place. Our package comes with ASD as part of that growth, and I'm OK with that."

As a matter of fact, this has helped to answer some questions I used to have and would put it in the "Lamar is so weird" category. Now, with the help of therapy, books, and you teaching me more about who you are, I'm able to understand the "weird." And believe it or not, it's teaching me so many things about myself as well. Is it a challenge? Yes, but it's also helping me to grow.

I especially liked how in one of your articles you talked about just seeing or recognizing that a coin has two sides and having the ability to see the other perspective. That was really an eye-opener for me, because I think we say this all the time about so many things. But in reality, living it can be hard because we're always thinking that only our perspective is the "right" one. I have to confess that I am not always right, and you aren't "weird."

We're just wired differently, and I know we complement each other well as we continue on the journey. And it can only get better.

There isn't a day that goes by that I don't think to myself, "Wow, when I was doing this or when I responded like that to Lamar, I had no idea how much I was stretching you beyond your comfort zone." I want you to know I *am really sorry from the bottom of my heart. I read and re-read your articles you've written for The Mighty, and I sometimes think about encounters we had. And it makes me realize how small I really was in some of those situations. I want you to know my ignorance to you being on the spectrum isn't an excuse, but your confirmed diagnosis has permanently removed all my ignorance. And it's teaching me so many ways that I can find the right balance in making your journey and our journey together everything I believe God intended for it to be.*

I love you so much, and my life would not be the same if you weren't a part of it! #youarestrong #youareawesome #youaregreat[1]

I've always been autistic. I just didn't discover the language to describe my neurology until I was well into adulthood. Learning that I had a developmental disability that had gone undiagnosed for over three decades was an experience that changed my life forever. Among the many things that I had to consider, I found myself most often wondering how disclosing my diagnosis to the world would change how people saw me. Receiving a diagnosis later in life proved to be challenging, because by the time you're thirty-six your personality is pretty set. People become accustomed to interacting with you in a distinct way. That also means that people have already determined your worth and the value you have in their lives. A diagnosis like mine can't simply be reduced to medical discovery. No, what I experienced was a spiritual event that made me overly insecure about every detail of my life prior to my diagnosis. What have I missed? Who have I hurt? What if I only knew? My insecurities and questions didn't linger in the past. Many took up residence in the present. My questions quickly migrated from thoughts of past failures to considerations of the future: What is going to happen now? How are people going to relate to me after they learn I'm autistic? Will people see me as someone they could call a friend, mentor, leader, or pastor? When I reflect on why those questions were so important, I realize they were really about interrogating my desirability: *Is anyone going to want me anymore?*

Perhaps that's why my wife and I made her letter public. There are scores of disabled people who don't just feel *out of place* in this world; they feel *undesired* by the world. Sharing my wife's feelings about me helped to highlight that disabled people don't just want to be tolerated; they need to be desired. The Christian faith speaks vividly about desire when it describes the lengths to which God has gone in order to pursue humanity. Christianity does not teach that God shows love by putting up with us. Instead, God's love is shown by displaying his desire for creation. Therefore, it is crucial that we address one of ableism's most significant abuses against disabled bodies.

A God Who Desires the Disabled

In November 2021, my social media feeds started flooding with private messages about an episode of the *Desiring God* podcast in which pastor John Piper addressed a question about beauty and attractiveness.

For those who may not be familiar with Piper, he is a popular pastor-theologian and founder of the Desiring God Ministries. His father was an itinerant evangelist, and his mother died in 1974 in a bus accident while visiting Israel. At Wheaton College (1964–68), he majored in literature and minored in philosophy. Following college, Piper completed a bachelor of divinity degree at Fuller Theological Seminary, where he discovered the writings of Jonathan Edwards. He did his doctoral work in New Testament studies at the University of Munich in West Germany (1971–74). In 1980, sensing an irresistible call to preach, he became the senior pastor of Bethlehem Baptist Church in Minneapolis, Minnesota, where he ministered for almost thirty-three years. Desiring God began in 1994 as a part of the church's tape ministry and has grown into an international web ministry with more than twelve thousand free resources and three and a half million monthly users. Piper serves as the lead teacher and content creator for Desiring God.[2]

Before we proceed, I need to be clear that Piper is not the subject of this chapter so much as a representative of modern Christian ideas about beauty and desirability. His response represents a much larger view. It exposes the influence of desire and attractiveness in contemporary culture—also known as *desirability politics*. Desirability politics suggests that the social ideals of beauty and attractiveness shape systems of power and control and quite often lead to intentional or unintentional oppression. The closer one is to being found desirable by social standards, the more access they have to resources, power, and privileges that make their life easier. Conversely, the further away a person is from being considered attractive and desirable by society, the further away they become from access to resources and opportunities to better their lives.

Desirability and attractiveness are not always merely about physical appearance. But more often than not, they significantly shape how we are taught to treat people. Disability, skin color, gender, sexual identity, weight, education, and even nationality are all factors that determine a person's desirability. Unfortunately, this system is often part of the framework for the practice of evangelical faith, and it stands as a stark contrast to the framework that moves disability and racial inclusion from being possible to being a priority.

Desirability politics shows up in the question submitted to Piper. In a heart-wrenching plea for help, the anonymous person reached out to him as a trusted source to help address why God would allow some people to be born unattractive. The person goes on to explain the challenges that many who feel unattractive encounter on a daily basis. The challenges range from encountering the sneers from a stranger secretly judging them to not being taken seriously in the workplace. Not surprisingly, the anonymous person has put a lot of thought into this challenge, especially from a theological perspective. They even go so far as to name the places in Scripture where people are described as beautiful. In the end, they want to know why God would place the burden of unattractiveness on any human body.

Piper opens his answer to the question by saying the following:

> When I hear a question like this, it makes me groan, partly because I can count on three fingers, maybe less, the people who have ever called me *ugly* or *handsome*. In other words, I groan because I know I'm being asked to speak to a sorrow that I've never tasted. It would be so much easier for

me to just ignore this question, because I know that when I'm done, many people would have the right to say, "But you've never experienced this." And that's true. Another reason it makes me groan to hear a question like this is that I know that what this person calls *ugly* is the tip of the iceberg of human suffering when it comes, for example, to horrific deformities—the kinds of dreadful disfigurements that in another age would be exploited in what were often advertised as "human freak shows." And then there are the kinds of diseases that produce hideous malformations and growths and cankerous, open, unhealable flesh. Then there are ghastly wounds that leave a person in pain the rest of their lives—*disabled, unsightly.*[3]

Piper engages the question by acknowledging that he has no experience with being regarded as unattractive, but he believes that what was presented as a question of attractiveness and beauty is only a surface issue that is actually related to human suffering. In other words, questions about ugliness—as determined by cultural ideals and values—are ultimately, Piper says, questions about suffering. Piper acknowledges the caller's pain, and the pain of others who may find themselves in similar circumstances. My focus in the next paragraphs is not on the validity of his argument but on the closing comment where he equates disability with unsightliness.

For most disability rights advocates, this closing comment is where Piper makes a critical error. He assumes that to be disabled means that a person cannot possess beauty. In doing this, he makes disability a placeholder for ugliness. This approach makes attractiveness exclusive to those who are able-bodied, meaning that the only quality necessary for assessing beauty is the ability to avoid what is seen as abnormality. Second, Piper assumes that disability equals suffering. It is true that living with a disability has its share of challenges, but many in the disability community loathe the idea that somehow their lives are a tragedy to be avoided. There are many people with disabilities who live thriving, fulfilling, and impactful lives that are far from the types of tropes Piper is presenting. Disability does not equal suffering and despair, nor does it mean that one cannot possess beauty.

We've all seen graphics of the large iceberg floating in water with arrows and captions pointing to the tip of the iceberg, while other arrows and captions point to and describe what is happening beneath the surface. Piper's point here highlights the iceberg of assumptions below the surface term *ugly*. Beneath the word are thoughts and discussions taking place deep beneath the surface of Western culture, including the Western church. If the tip of the iceberg is the lack of beauty, then the bottom of the iceberg, the base for the argument against the ugly and the undesirable, is a connection to disability. Piper's perspective is posed as an answer to a question, but in reality, his perspective—and the predominant perspective of evangelical Christians—raises more questions than it answers. What is beauty? What is the relationship between beauty and faith? Who determines eligibility for occupying this space called beautiful? Who are the gatekeepers who guard the "godly" land of beauty, attractiveness, and desire?

The politics of desire often begins with laying the weight of insecurity at the feet of those who often feel displaced in a culture that has deemed them ugly or undesirable. But what if we began the discussion of desirability in a different place? The evangelical response to feelings of being ugly is commonly the use of spiritual sleight of hand to actually affirm the ugliness of those questioning their beauty. Rather than addressing the anonymous caller's concerns of feeling ugly, Piper does what we often do. He names other expressions of ugliness and groups them all together into a category he describes as suffering. His response illustrates the ways that being judged for one's appearance is an accepted part of our society.

This does nothing to ease the insecurity of the many people who already feel undesirable. You can hear the pain in the caller's words when they ask why God would allow them to exist in a world that considers them both undesirable and ungodly. This is typical of ableism: ableism stands at the gate of beauty and guards those who are deemed undesirable from gaining entry.

What if insecurity for being ugly or undesirable is not a punishment but a prophetic push against the unholy ableist practice of gatekeeping beauty and desire? Da'Shaun Harrison writes, "Insecurities are often taught as something to be afraid of, to be ashamed of, to run away from. People are taught that the way they feel about their bodies is their own moral failing and therefore their responsibility to hold. We are all often socialized into believing that if we are insecure, then we are weak, incapable, or ugly and that all of these things are bad things to be."[4] Harrison believes that instead of scrutinizing individuals who are insecure about their beauty or their bodies, insecurity serves to critique a social system that punishes people for failing to live up to superficial standards.

The connection between Harrison's theory and Christianity is that most Christians believe any form of imperfection or suffering that exists in the world is the direct result of the initial sin of Adam and Eve. In his response, Piper goes on to make this connection by quoting from Romans 8:18–20, saying, "This is a reference to the fall in Genesis 3, the fall into sin and the consequent miseries that were brought into the world—all the horrific consequences of sin, including every disfigurement, every injury, every disability, every catastrophe."[5] Connecting disability, injury, disfigurement, and all other manner of unattractiveness to sin, is for many Christians, a direct link to moral failing. In doing this, Piper uses ugliness (and disability) as a placeholder for sin and makes insecurities about a lack of beauty a matter of morality. Rather than addressing the caller's insecurities about their lack of beauty, Piper frames his response in a way that reinforces the insecurity as valid according to societal standards.

A person's insecurity is not an isolated incident of image distortion. For a person to feel insecure about their looks, their weight, their disability, and so on, they have to have come to that conclusion based on external definitions of beauty. Piper and teachers like him show the ongoing need to address how ableism and racism are embedded in our collective psyche in ways that affect nearly every facet of our society and culture.

Racism is often reduced to individual acts of hatred, rather than viewed as institutionally driven ways of seeing the world. In the same way, the politics of beauty has been reduced to a person's individual struggle with their own image. The caller who reached out to Piper and his ministry is not simply lamenting the idea of being unattractive because their appearance has troubled them. They are expressing the type of anxiety that surfaces when society transmits image insecurity onto them because they fail to meet a set standard of beauty—of what a normal and desired body looks like. Very often, the price for failing to live up to this standard is public shame, stigma, and bearing the weight of feeling undesired.

What Piper fails to address in his response, and what our society continues to ignore, is that people want to be wanted. Our deepest desire isn't to be tolerated; it is to be desired and pursued.

At worst, Piper's answer reinforces an unwillingness to give all bodies access to beauty and desirability. In the world of disability ministry, we call this "accommodation," but I have to believe that accommodating people with disabilities—or better yet, accommodating people who don't fit neatly packaged, idealized versions of human existence—is not the goal. Accommodation isn't the holy grail of the gospel of disability. Accommodation is the floor, and honestly, it isn't even a nice floor; it's just a nice-enough floor to build our theology of disability, desirability, and beauty on. God shows up by desiring. He expresses that desire most intently through pursuit. Ableism in American evangelical spaces exists because it doesn't beckon the church to pursue the disabled, let alone to desire them.

The Ugly Laws

I have served in a variety of ministry roles for more than two decades. Of all the ways I've had the opportunities to serve, the most impactful placement was as a hospice chaplain.

The academy introduced me to chaplaincy as a first-year seminary student. As part of our educational experience, the school placed students in ministry internships for about six hours a week. I was assigned to a local hospice in Atlanta as my contextual education site. I hated it. I felt ill-prepared, unqualified, and overwhelmed with being tasked to support persons and families facing life-limiting illnesses. I completed my required year of residency but vowed never to return to hospice ministry again.

Several years later, I would return to hospice chaplaincy, and the second time around, my experience was completely different. To this day, I attribute much of my spiritual growth and pastoral philosophy to my time spent as a hospice chaplain.

My work with hospice often meant that someone asked me to take part in funerals for the patients I spent time with. Occasionally, I would act in my capacity as a spiritual advisor for these individuals over extended periods, which allowed us to form a deep bond, deep enough to be asked to deliver a eulogy. Countless experiences shaped me during this time, but perhaps no service shaped my life more than the funeral service I conducted at a patient's home with his entire family present.

The service had an informal beginning. There was no procession. No reading of the Twenty-Third Psalm. No liturgy. Our time together simply began when the son of my patient gathered us together to share his feelings about his father. I'll always remember the way he began his story. "The best way to talk about my dad is to start not by telling all that he was. The best way to describe my father is to start by telling everything that he *wasn't.*"

When it comes to beauty, I have often felt as though definitions of what is desirable often begin with traits that don't belong—that is, beauty is frequently determined by describing what is *not* beautiful. If a person has any type of perceived deficit, or a body that is considered atypical, they are usually considered to be unattractive.

This principle has been codified into American law. Ableism and attractiveness have a long-standing connection in our national history. As one example, in the late 1800s, cities began passing ordinances aimed at reducing the number of "unsightly beggars" in their communities. The term *unsightly* was a euphemism for disability, particularly physical disabilities that people deemed offensive.

The site of the longest-standing set of what would eventually become known as "ugly laws" in the country was San Francisco. In 1867, the city introduced a subset of laws designed to discourage street begging. The ordinance born out of the begging laws included two separate indiscretions: one was street begging, the other loitering on the streets of the city and in public places. Police could enforce the law if they caught a person begging, or if a person met the criteria that defined the "certain people" prohibited from appearing publicly, or if a person fell into both categories.

By adding stipulations about "certain people" to the begging ordinance, San Francisco effectively passed a law that attached disability to definitions of beauty and attractiveness. This made it unlawful for "any person who is diseased, maimed, mutilated, or in any way deformed"[6] to appear in public. Chicago and New Orleans would implement their own versions of ugly laws. These laws treated disability as an undesirable eyesore that tarnished the value and reputations of cities that sought to bolster their social and economic standings.

Christianity doesn't explicitly purport any ugly laws as part of its religious doctrine, but it could be argued that far too often Western Christianity's version of ugly laws lives in its unchecked use of rhetoric that associates both disability and Blackness with the most undesirable status a person can occupy. Not all churches struggle with this issue; however, there are a significant number of Christians and churches that unknowingly use disability-related language to describe undesirable conditions. I was once asked my opinion about a popular pastor and speaker's repeated use of the word "lame" in a sermon to describe people who make excuses for not following God's plan for their life. I'm almost certain that his use of the word was meant to be a rhetorical device developed from using the actual word in the biblical text regarding the story of the man at the pool of Bethesda (John 5:1–15). The challenge is that using disability language as a synonym for an undesirable condition can be extremely harmful. Using terms such as lame, blind, paralyzed, darkness, black, and the like while attaching it to undesirable conditions is just one of the ways that churches unintentionally cause spiritual harm.

In the modern American evangelical movement, every weekend worshipers file into beautiful buildings with manicured lawns built on land that was transformed from being bare and full of untapped potential into pristine places of worship. The smell of coffee and baked goods supplements the subtle messaging of beauty and attractiveness, as state-of-the-art technology breathes life into our gatherings while we gaze upon musicians and ministers who sing beautifully, always on key, while simultaneously faithfully showing a firm grasp of fashion, often sporting the latest styles and the hottest retro sneakers.

Our churches love beauty. We create cue sheets each week for the worship experience because we need a comprehensive strategy for moving through worship in a way that eliminates distractions. Transitions must be smooth and seamless. Sound and lighting have to be on point. We use in-ear monitors and click tracks to ensure that the entire band stays on pace with the musical programming for the morning. We mark the stage with tape, showing where every person should stand so that the camera angles are just right as the stage lights hit the soloist, projecting their good side. We do all this so that from week to week and month to month, people have an experience that is void of messiness. No mistakes. No missteps. No distractions. Nothing unattractive.

Striving for a mistake-free service isn't bad. Desiring to experience beauty isn't bad. The challenge is that beauty is an abstract concept. Our inability to define beauty without using a deficit model stands in contrast to our fundamental beliefs about how God created us. Our origin begins outside of us. An infinitely holy and wise God who creates with intention and intimacy placed us in the world. Acknowledging God's creative genius challenges us to believe that God does not create anything that is not beautiful in its own way.

I connect the challenge of defining beauty to the problem of origin. Beauty has to begin somewhere. Understanding something as abstract as beauty requires the ability to traverse through the annals of time and arrive at the standard or the starting point of beauty. As created beings, we simply don't have that ability or the authority to do so. Most of our working definitions of beauty tend to be superficial, which explains why the standards can often change depending on culture and context. I've found that definitions of beauty are often formed from the perspectives of those who have the most power. Those who have power also usually have the influence and financial means to promote and market a particular look, hairstyle, skin tone, height, and the like as the apex of human beauty.

The Politics of Desire and Ability

The politics of desire and ability is most often experienced at the intersection of disability and Blackness. We built this nation by using segregation as the primary gatekeeping mechanism for attaining social capital. We used desire and ability as the template for creating the first social category that experienced exemption from social mobility and social and political capital. In their book *On the Politics of Ugliness*, Ela Przybylo and Sara Rodrigues describe how both beauty and desire operate as gatekeepers in the Western world. They write, "Ugliness or unsightliness is much more than a quality or property of an individual's appearance—it has long functioned as a social category that demarcates access to social, cultural, and political spaces. People who are unsightly are framed as not only unworthy of being seen or of having eyes set upon them, but they then become the target of interventions to curb the possibility of their causing aversion and discomfort in others."[7]

In the United States, many cities used ugly law ideology to support ableism, racism, and classism. Ugly laws and the politics of desire and ability played a significant role in the shaping of a social order that would place disability and Blackness on the bottom rung of the ladder. Desire/ability politics as a system for subordinating certain image bearers is a Christian problem. It is a Christian problem because it is a subtle smothering of the creative power of God, whose imagination invented a variety of bodies, including Black bodies and disabled bodies. The politics of desire/ability developed in concert with ugly laws, which were developed within the context of racial slavery, segregation, and other laws that helped to support them.

Christian charity has also played a role in influencing who is viewed as deserving of care. Early Western Christian concepts of charity assigned a permanent state of incompetence and inequality to those who received support. In fact, charity, as practiced historically, had links to what we now call eugenics because it was believed that charity was a system that encouraged the flourishing of a community of undesirables, and this called into question the goal of charitable giving.

In the nineteenth century, pastor and sociologist Charles Henderson (1848–1915) popularized a new way of practicing charity by asserting that charity should never be indiscriminate. He taught that almsgiving and charity needed a set of standards that eliminated the survival of an undesirable class of citizens. Henderson believed that giving needed to be informed by a clear and standard definition of what a "normal person" is. While he acknowledged that an image of normality could never be exact, he challenged the intellectuals of his day to use science to devise such an image that was as exact as science could be.[8] The scientific and, frequently, spiritual creation of what it means to be a normal human created a standard that permeated the practice of Christian charity, intentionally linked able-bodiedness to images of the ideal, and defended the need for a eugenic form of charity, a charity that makes Western Christianity exclusive to non-Black, nondisabled bodies.

The Consequence of False Images

Returning to the book of Judges (17:1–6), the initial sin of Micah is theft, a sin he is not held accountable for. Instead, Micah takes the idols his mother has made for him and turns his home into a shrine, complete with a sacred ephod and some other household idols. He also makes his son his personal priest. Just these few verses expose us to his perpetual indiscretions, and yet, unfortunately, this is far from the end of the story.

One day, a Levite from Bethlehem arrives in the area and stops at Micah's house as he is searching for a place to live. When Micah finds out where he is from and what his occupation is, he offers the man a place to stay, but in a strange twist in the text, he offers the Levite a job as his personal priest with an annual salary and benefits. Shockingly, the Levite accepts the job offer. The closing lines of chapter 17 read like an eerie foreshadowing of the failure of the religious community. "'I know the LORD will bless me now,' Micah said, 'because I have a Levite serving as my priest'" (Judg. 17:13). Spoiler alert: things do not go well for Micah. All of his idols are eventually stolen, his priest abandons him, and Micah's life is threatened. Eventually, he ends up with nothing. What's worse, the tribe that has stolen Micah's idols ends up forcefully and violently taking over a town from peaceful people, renaming the town, and setting up a tabernacle of God using Micah's idols as the objects of their worship. The initial sin of Micah, the creation of idols by his mother, and his attempts to use religion to cover his tracks, end up having both generational and geographical consequences.

The consequences of creating false images extends beyond the motivation that inspired their creation. As in the story of Micah, American Christianity has used religion to cover the tracks of its initial sin only to watch the ungodly images that it created grow into an entire system that attached itself to the tabernacle—that is, the church. Images of beauty and notions about which humans have the best bodies is an egregious sin that has seduced the church and impacted the practice of Western Christian faith. We, too, are recipients of the consequences of the theft of African bodies—namely, the ableism and racism that have taught our tribe to worship false images, images that alienate God and oppress God's people. The politics of desire and ability is a dangerous collection of ideals that taint the tabernacle and threaten the faith. In order to better understand just how pervasive and persuasive these idols have been, we will need to examine key moments of ableism in the history of Christianity.

Do No Harm

Religious Rhetoric, Disability, and Healthcare

I've always had a complicated history with the healthcare system. When I was younger, I experienced painful leg and lower body spasms that would incapacitate me for hours. I remember having an episode in elementary school that was so bad that my friends had to carry me home from the playground. These attacks came often at night, and I would cry out loudly because the pain was so excruciating. I can even recall my mother coming into my bedroom at night to pray that the episodes would subside and the pain would go away. These mysterious challenges never had a name. No label to help me understand what my body was doing to me. I was once told that I was a carrier for the sickle cell gene, a common trait for many Black people, but carrying the trait didn't explain my symptoms.

Over the years, I have suffered from debilitating migraine headaches. I can trace the genesis of these headaches back to my late teenage years. Initially, I concluded that they came from lack of sleep or stress, but as the years went on, I failed to find any adequate relief by adjusting my lifestyle. The headaches continued for years, showing up at least weekly. During this time, I had what seemed like every possible medical test done to try to pinpoint the cause. Scans, blood work, stress tests, blood pressure checks, dental exams, and the like failed to lead to a diagnosis of any kind.

Both my strange episodes of lower body pain and the recurring migraines remain two of the most mysterious medical ailments that I have experienced. Nothing is quite as frustrating as being in pain and not having an answer about the cause. Throughout the years, I've found various ways to deal with both of these issues, and for the most part, neither one has been as troubling as it was in the past. Still, I've yet to receive any real answers about my medical problems. Well, except one. My problems had to be related to something I was doing or something I was taking or something I was ingesting. At least that's what multiple doctors led me to believe. Whatever was causing these issues, one thing was clear: I always went away feeling judged about my lack of care for my body, even though I had absolutely no clue what I could have possibly done wrong. Neither did the doctors, for that matter; however, this didn't stop them from believing what has long been believed about both disabled bodies and Black bodies, which is that pain and suffering are part and parcel of a body that is perceived as flawed and morally inferior.

This became even more of a reality for me when, in 2023, I was sent home from the emergency department of a local hospital twice after having some severe abdominal pain misdiagnosed. Upon the first trip to the emergency room, I was sent home without any pain medication. The second trip to the emergency room was by ambulance just four days later, with the same issue and increased pain. The doctors at the hospital never considered my history of rectal cancer with its associated treatments and surgeries. I was treated as a drug-seeking patient and sent home without adequate answers or relief from my excruciating pain. Eventually, my wife took me to the emergency department of the hospital where I was being treated for cancer. It was there that I was told that I had a large bowel obstruction due to scar tissue from previous cancer treatment and that my colon was in danger of rupturing and causing septic shock. I needed emergency surgery. I would end up spending six days in the hospital recovering from a major medical issue, which two other doctors told me was mere constipation.

In this chapter, I'll show how a distorted version of Christianity often practiced in America bares significant blame for linking Blackness to disability. This means that as the nation was being formed, the belief that Black bodies are inherently disabled or unwell allowed for Black people to be treated as medically unstable people. In other words, Blackness itself became a medical issue. To be Black meant to be unwell, which allowed for the dismissal of all types of medical ailments that Black people faced because they were just expected to be medically unhealthy as a race of people. This is how ableism (and racism) has reared its ugly head in healthcare, and I am far from the only disabled or Black person to have had this experience.

How Religion and Race Began Defining Health

In the years preceding the Civil War, medical professionals in the South tried to build exclusive professional recognition in the medical field by distancing themselves from the medical practices of the North. This effort to distance themselves from Northern medical training centers was linked to Southern laws that upheld slavery. Southern doctors claimed to have a unique set of medical circumstances based on their large population of Blacks, rooted in what is called the medical model of disability. The medical model of disability insists that disability is the result of biomedical conditions that limit the bodies and minds of those deemed disabled.

The medical model of disability "pathologizes" individuals. To pathologize a person or a group of people is to view them as abnormal. Their bodies, behaviors, and even beliefs are considered abnormal or diseased, making it easy to see the whole person as medically unhealthy. They are seen according to conditions that make their bodies and minds abnormal or atypical. The pathologizing of Blackness and disability in Western medicine and science has a historical connection to religious rhetoric, rhetoric that has influenced the moralizing of medical issues most often related to the Black community.

Disability, then, has become a series of problems to be fixed or cured, thus placing the disabled at the mercy of the medical community. This approach to disability and Blackness provided the needed platform for Southern physicians to pathologize Blackness and, in doing so, to assert their superior knowledge of medicine. The messages that early Christian theology attached to disability and Blackness continue to be pervasive. Early Puritan theology paved the way for the fusing of morality with medical diagnoses and treatments in a manner that produced a healthcare system that had very little chance of operating without bias. What follows are examples of how certain historical figures have perpetuated these biases.

Cotton Mather

Cotton Mather was a clergyman who lived from 1663 to 1728. He was a third-generation Puritan minister and theologian. Mather was born into an affluent New England family and, following his graduation from Harvard, became the pastor of a church in the northern part of Boston. Mather's life was drastically shaped by continuous health challenges. Thirteen of his fifteen children preceded him in death. Illness took the lives of both his first wife and his second wife. Even his third wife was known to have some form of mental illness. As a result of his experiences with illness and death, Mather became obsessed with making sense of suffering and illness and taking on the task of more closely examining the causes of sickness and looking for remedies.

Mather's quest to answer questions surrounding suffering and illness was heavily shaped by American Puritan theology. Author Heather H. Vacek, in her book *Madness: American Protestant Responses to Mental Illness*, writes, "Mather understood all things—life, death, illness, health, nature, and humanity—theologically, and that shaped his exploration of the purpose and causes of sickness. Rarely did his writing separate sickness and theological reflection."[1] Mather believed that mental and physical illnesses need not be classified as different types of illness. Like many in his day, he believed that mental and physical illnesses were essentially the same. In fact, Mather believed that all people suffered from varying degrees of what he called "mental distress."

Mather spent most of his life and career providing what he believed to be critical insight into the medical field. In 1724, he would write a medical journal called *The Angel of Bethesda*, which was published after his death. At the time, his journal was the only comprehensive medical journal in the colonial period. It explored various physical and mental illnesses while providing medical and theological insight into the causes of and cures for a number of ailments. Vacek writes, "That a clergyman authored a medical volume shows the authoritative role religious leaders played in a wide range of arenas during the colonial era."[2] Mather's work is an example of how, very early on, the American healthcare system was influenced by clergy who convinced the populace that a person's moral standing had a direct impact on their medical health.

Dr. John Harvey Kellogg

John Harvey Kellogg is best known for founding the Kellogg cereal empire alongside his brother, Will Keith Kellogg. He was born into a family that held disdain for how medicine was practiced. According to records, his father, John Preston Kellogg, was instrumental in convincing James and Ellen White, prominent figures in the founding of the

Seventh-day Adventist Church, to relocate to Battle Creek, Michigan, to expand their movement. They believed that sickness of any kind was a punishment and a reminder from God that people were abusing their bodies. Among the necessary responses to this punishment was adopting a vegetarian diet as a way to purify the body of disease and disability. Because the young John Harvey was raised to believe the principles of Seventh-day Adventism, when he reached adulthood, the leaders of the church wanted him to take on a larger role as a teacher and educator about issues related to health. According to author and scholar Sabrina Strings, "Kellogg was a major player in the increasing encroachment of medicine into questions of the proper diet and weight for the average American, a terrain previously dominated by race scientists and religious reformers. Rather than skirting or directly rejecting ethno-religious theories of the links between race, femininity, weight, and health, John Harvey Kellogg, a physician, eugenicist, and ardent Christian, combined [them]."[3]

Kellogg was eventually asked to step down from church leadership because his occupation as a surgeon was seen as distracting him from his call to ministry. Kellogg would not only step down; he would also split from the leadership of the church, although he still helmed the denomination's mental health facility. After leaving the church, Kellogg increased his efforts at leveraging his medico-religious beliefs to influence health reform; however, he was now free to develop a system for standardizing health practices that would ensure the survival of the White race. Kellogg was a eugenicist, and like many eugenicists of his day, he believed that Black people were genetically inferior and that, due to the residue of slavery and the climate produced by Jim Crow, they were headed toward extinction.

Kellogg turned his focus toward what is now known as "biological living," a version of healthcare that sought to maintain the superior status of White people by teaching them principles of health, which included everything from who they should procreate with to what they should eat, how much exercise they should get, and how much they should weigh. While Kellogg's specific focus was on improving the health of White women as a way to ensure the propagation of the White race, Kellogg's influence led to the acceptance of his ideas by mainstream American medicine. Some of today's standards of health were born out of Kellogg's desire to preserve the status, stature, and supremacy of the White race, and accordingly, a definition of health evolved that excludes both Black and disabled bodies. Both Kellogg's profession as a doctor and his influence in the religious world gave him the credibility to create a race-based standard of health that continues to exert influence in the present day.

Anton Boisen

The early 1920s saw a new form of theological training now known as clinical pastoral education (CPE). CPE was born out of the risk-taking endeavors of Dr. William A. Bryan (1883–1944), superintendent of Worcester State Hospital, when he hired Rev. Anton Boisen (1876–1965) as the hospital chaplain.[4]

Boisen was once diagnosed with schizophrenia, and it is reported that over the course of fifteen years, he had at least five severe psychotic episodes. His frequent hospitalizations prompted him to pay keen attention to issues of mental health and disability. He felt called to lead the church to play a larger role in diagnosing and treating the mentally and physically disabled. In 1924, Boisen was appointed to a faculty position at Chicago Theological Seminary. During his twenty-year tenure there, he advocated for the return of church authority and clergy oversight in medical matters, including mental and physical disabilities.

At a time when medicine was moving away from the influence of Christian thought and theology, Boisen had a tremendous influence on clergy reclaiming religious authority in medical care. With the return of clerical influence came perspectives about medical conditions that were closely linked to embedded Christian views about the source of mental or physical disabilities. While physicians led the way in defining illness in general and mental disabilities in particular, the ongoing influence of religion in the medical profession led to the moralization of medical issues.

Boisen's CPE model emerged as a system that clerically endorsed psychiatric techniques and other medical procedures. The process for endorsement was to have chaplains in medical facilities assist in the care of the mentally or physically disabled. While the goal was to have clergy and physicians work together, the influence of religion on medical care ultimately meant accepting the influence of religious definitions of moral behavior, definitions that often led to the evaluation of patients' conditions in light of Christian ideals. In 1940, some mental health facilities began hiring part-time chaplains or allowing local clergy to hold church services in their facilities. Despite cooperation from some physicians and reports that religious services had a positive

71

impact on patients, there were still debates about the possibility of clergy involvement weakening the authority of physicians. Like Mather and Kellogg, Boisen's influence still lingers in our current medical practices today. Perceptions about moral behavior continue to have an influence over how Black bodies are evaluated and treated.

This Is Why Black People Die

Chaniece Wallace was a fourth-year pediatric chief resident at the Indiana University School of Medicine. Wallace was thirty-five weeks pregnant with a baby girl when she began to develop symptoms associated with preeclampsia.[5] Preeclampsia is a serious medical condition that can occur around the midpoint of a pregnancy. It causes high blood pressure, protein in the urine, swelling, headaches, and blurred vision. It can also affect other organs and is often extremely dangerous for the mother and the unborn child. Preeclampsia is usually diagnosed during routine prenatal appointments.[6]

When Wallace developed signs of preeclampsia, doctors decided to deliver her baby via C-section. While the baby was delivered successfully, Wallace suffered from complications, including a ruptured liver, a lack of kidney function, and high blood pressure, all of which required her to have additional surgeries. She died just four days after the birth of her daughter.[7]

In a story about Wallace, Joelle Goldstein cites a Centers for Disease Control and Prevention report that Black women are two to three times more likely to die from pregnancy-related causes than White women.[8] Dr. Lauren

Dungy-Poythress, a maternal-fetal medicine specialist at Indiana University, remarked about Wallace's case, "Preeclampsia can present any way it wants to. . . . But the question is, do Black mothers get the care or scrutiny that they need?" This article goes on to report that "racial disparities in maternal mortality outcomes may occur in part because of the chronic stresses that people of color endure from discrimination, which can take a toll on their health. . . . 'You can be a healthy Black woman and still have a higher risk of maternal mortality,' Dungy-Poythress said. 'What [Dr. Wallace's death] unfortunately highlights is that it's not based on access to care.'"[9] The data conveying the disproportionate deaths among Black women suggests that the healthcare system is still deficient in its care for them.

Another young Black woman, Shalon Irving, had ascended the ranks at the Center for Disease Control and Prevention (CDC) by the age of thirty-six. As an epidemiologist, Irving was trying to understand the role structural inequalities play in public health. According to her mentor at the CDC, she wanted to expose both how limited health options led to poor health outcomes in Black communities and the victim blaming that arose from biases against lower income communities and communities of color.[10] Like Wallace, Irving gave birth to a child and, three weeks later, died of complications related to high blood pressure. In an ironic twist, the public health official who had worked to eradicate healthcare disparities became another case study in those very disparities facing Black women in the United States.

The stories of Wallace, Irving, and other Black women in America demonstrate how history has led to the pathologizing of Blackness. Pathology is the study of disease. It is a way to study things that operate abnormally within the human body. To pathologize a person or a group of people is to treat them as abnormal. Their bodies, behaviors, and even beliefs are considered abnormal or diseased, making it easy to see the whole person as medically unhealthy. An example of pathologizing Blackness was the creation in 1851 of a diagnosis called drapetomania, which supposedly explained the cause of slaves continually attempting to flee captivity. Because Blacks were considered abnormal, their belief that they should be free was not seen as a moral issue but rather a medical one.

What I experienced in being misdiagnosed, and what countless others have experienced in being dismissed, illustrates how the medical establishment saw medical issues as moral failings. If we had just taken better care of ourselves or didn't have preexisting conditions, then we would have avoided our respective medical challenges. When being Black itself is seen as abnormal and unhealthy, it becomes doubly difficult to have your needs taken seriously.

Race, Health, and Body Types

Early on, Puritan values in America presented an ideal body type that served as a standard for health and well-being. These concepts of what it meant to be healthy were rooted in racial and disability discrimination. Eventually, these views even led to the development of healthcare as a strategy for maintaining White supremacy in the aftermath of the Civil War.[11]

The view that Blackness was inherently unhealthy directly contributed to the racializing of certain body types.

The racializing of health happens when a person's race is seen as the primary factor that determines their health. It is a way to designate people to categories of health and wellness based on their race and not on medical evidence. When Black bodies are deemed unhealthy regardless of their medical status, this can lead to assumptions among medical practitioners that any medical issue that a Black person has is first a result of them being Black.

In 2021, the popular television series *Grey's Anatomy* addressed this issue in an episode titled "Some Kind of Tomorrow," in which doctors discover that a scientifically inaccurate test has been preventing Black patients from receiving kidney transplants because the test is rooted in assumptions about Black bodies that are simply untrue. While this story takes place in a fictitious medical drama, the harsh reality is that it is indeed a case of art imitating life. According to a report from USA Today, "The current most widely used test to estimate kidney function—estimated glomerular filtration rate or eGFR test—uses creatinine, a waste product in the blood created by muscle use, to calculate how well kidneys are working. Black people in original studies to develop the test may have had nonbiological exposures that affected creatinine levels, such as medications or dietary differences—but scientists, trying to account for these differences seen in Black participants, deduced Black people had more 'muscle mass,' so had a higher baseline level of creatinine."[12]

Researchers have since debunked this racial myth, pointing out that Black bodies do not have kidneys that function differently than those of any other race. There is simply no scientific evidence to substantiate these claims. The report goes on to explain that "the antiquated calculation systematically raises estimated kidney function by as much as 16% for Black people compared with patients of all other racial groups, conferring an estimate of better kidney function for Black individuals."[13] Not surprisingly, some in the medical profession have attempted to justify the continued use of this formula, arguing that it suggests that Black kidney function is healthier than that of their White counterparts. The problem with this view and similar false narratives about Black bodies is, of course, the reality that Black bodies can never escape this designation. This has meant that Black people who have actually needed medical intervention in the form of a kidney transplant have been denied access to the donor list because of an unfounded myth about the way their bodies function. "We know that race can really introduce implicit bias into the clinical encounter, and we know that there are studies that have shown implicit bias has negatively affected Black individuals," says Dr. Nwamaka D. Eneanya, an author of a recent *New England Journal of Medicine* study that has produced an inclusive equation. "Hopefully, the way forward is that we won't have any tools that lead with race or ethnicity, that we'll have real measures of structural racism."[14]

We should remember that the racialization of health has also included versions of beauty that have been anti-Black. These accounts include disability and weight as factors that determine beauty, hence contributing to anti-Blackness.[15] In addition to disability, fatness, and abnormal body types being central to anti-Blackness, ideas about desirability and physical attractiveness contribute to the problem of racialized healthcare. Healthcare becomes another arena where "abnormal" bodies are subjugated for not meeting contrived standards.

A New Narrative about Disability and Health

Blackness, health, and disability have been historically linked to religious rhetoric and Christian rituals. This has led to a narrative about health that is steeped in moral and religious values. This narrative has also led to barriers to adequate healthcare for Blacks and for those with disabilities. Constructing a new narrative about health, disability, and race requires a critique of previous narratives. Why are certain minority communities more susceptible to particular health issues? Why does colorectal cancer disproportionately affect the Black community? Black people are about 20 percent more likely to get colorectal cancer and about 40 percent more likely to die from it than almost any other group. Why is that? Does being Black make me more likely to get cancer? Or does being Black make me less likely to have access to information about testing and access to treatment? Historically, the answer to these questions would have been simply that Black bodies are inherently unhealthy and inherently disabled. In addition, the disproportionate number of Black people dying from colorectal cancer would have been attributed to moral failings rather than a society's failure to provide equal access to early detection and treatment.

We also have to grapple with the historic connection between race, health, and disability that promoted the need for healthy Black bodies for labor and production on plantations. Healthcare in that system of thinking was not

considered a human right for Black bodies but an obligation owed to their owners. This long history of health as
an obligation has also made it difficult for Black bodies to
exist in the world apart from their obligation to provide
something of value. Sonya Taylor writes in her book *The
Body Is Not an Apology*, "Health is not a state we owe the
world. We are not less valuable, worthy, or lovable, because
we are not healthy. Lastly, there is no standard of health that
is achievable for all bodies."[16]

Constructing a new narrative about race, disability, health,
and religion also requires placing the dialogue within the
broader, ongoing discussion about social justice in America.
This can include incorporating the philosophy of Dr. Martin
Luther King Jr. into the conversation about how to build a
more equitable and more just narrative about health, disability, and race. Régine Michelle Jean-Charles, author of
Martin Luther King and "The Trumpet of Conscience" Today,
writes, "King's vision is not so distant from many of the activists and thinkers fighting injustice today, whether they be
leaders of the Black Lives Matter movement, anti-rape advocates, or prison abolitionists. When we read *The Trumpet
of Conscience* and focus on the more radical parts of his vision, the relevance of King's message still resonates today."[17]

King's voice, among many others of the civil rights movement, would most certainly help shape a quite different
narrative about Blackness, health, disability, and especially
the role of the church in advocating for equitable access
to healthcare. We forget that King was a radical Christian
minister who believed in the power of love and creativity.
King would have rebelled against the idea that Black bodies—or any bodies, for that matter—are inherently inferior,

mentally or physically. For King, that would be an insult to the God of creation, and while he is most known for one pivotal speech associated with the march on Washington, the King we should emulate was a radical believer in the power of God to move people toward personal and structural transformation.

Rebranding Health and Rebuilding Healthcare

On May 6, 2021, the US House Oversight and Reform Committee held a hearing on racism in Black maternal healthcare. Witnesses included scores of Black families whose mothers, sisters, and daughters had died giving birth. The maternal mortality rate among Black women is a crisis in the US healthcare system. Tina Suliman, of the Johns Hopkins Center for Communication Programs, had this to say:

> This crisis is driven by unconscious bias in the medical system and its actors. In a 2016 study of white medical students, nearly half held false beliefs about biological differences in Black patients, including thicker skin and less sensitive nerve endings. Another 2020 study found that Black babies are more likely to live if they are cared for by a Black physician. Recently, the CDC declared racism a public health threat. The maternal mortality crisis in the United States emphasizes the truth behind this declaration: It is racism, not race, that is killing America's Black mothers and babies.[18]

Suliman also reports that despite having expertise and even formal medical training, as Wallace and Irving did, Black mothers are often denied the right to define their own maternal health. The result is a lack of adequate medical intervention that could save the lives of many Black women.

Disparities in healthcare have impacted communities of color. There is no shortage of data that suggests that racism has played a significant role in shaping the healthcare system. According to the CDC, the body of research regarding racial bias in the healthcare system is growing. The current research indicates what is described as "profound and negative impacts on communities of color." The impact of racial bias in healthcare is deeply and destructively embedded in American society and culture. The CDC reports:

> The data show that racial and ethnic minority groups, throughout the United States, experience higher rates of illness and death across a wide range of health conditions, including diabetes, hypertension, obesity, asthma, and heart disease, when compared to their White counterparts. Additionally, the life expectancy of non-Hispanic/Black Americans is four years lower than that of White Americans. The COVID-19 pandemic and its disproportionate impact among racial and ethnic minority populations is another stark example of these enduring health disparities.[19]

Building a better healthcare experience for people of color ultimately means building a better story about Black bodies. In America, Blackness has been pathologized because of its historical connection to disability—connections that were initiated and influenced by religious traditions, particularly early colonial-era Christian churches.

Central to the effort to rebrand health is the need to examine strategies of organizations or social justice movements that have experienced success in changing the narrative about both Black and disabled bodies. The civil rights and disability rights movements share common strategies that are essential to this process. The first is the use of images in critiquing current narratives about disability and Blackness.

The genius of Dr. King's work as a civil rights leader is found in his ability to reconstruct the American narrative about Black bodies by providing an alternate vision of Black America and its relationship to the failed American dream of all people receiving equal treatment. His work provides a template for creating new images of Black and disabled bodies as worthy of respect and equality. Even King's most famous speech about dreams was a powerful move to guide America to embrace a competing image of Blackness, an image that required action against placing Black bodies on the bottom of the body hierarchy.

A new narrative is possible when notions of health are adequately critiqued. There are many activists who have taken on the mantle left behind by Dr. King and various other civil rights and disability rights leaders.

Insecurity as a Measurement for Institutional Racism and Ableism

The untimely deaths of Chaniece Wallace and Shalon Irving are representative of a systemic racist and ableist structure in American healthcare and in the American narrative about disability and Blackness. Their stories are case studies of all the ways that ableism has fueled racism in our healthcare system. They were two highly educated and accomplished Black women who did not fit the narrative of Black death as being a direct result of being unhealthy, uneducated, and poor. To the contrary, they transcended ableist and racist stereotypes only to still be denied the proper medical care they deserved because ableism insists that Black bodies are inherently unhealthy. For Black bodies seeking proper medical care, expressions of inadequate care are often relegated to feelings of insecurity about their bodies. This is also true of disabled bodies that are bound to a destructive narrative about body difference.

The influence of religion in healthcare has led to the moralization of medical issues. Terms such as *preexisting conditions* and *comorbidities* are often weaponized to measure the character of Black and disabled bodies. The challenge of being Black or disabled is the challenge of measuring up to a health standard that remains unattainable for bodies designated as deficient. Insecurity, then, is the result of institutional racism rather than the result of an individual lack of accountability for one's body. Insecurity is the tax that marginalized bodies pay for being pushed to the margins, which also means that insecurity can actually serve as a measurement for the degree to which institutional racism and ableism in healthcare are present.

When it comes to healthcare in America, bodies deemed normal are bodies that are most desirable. Understanding the politics of desire and beauty is an essential tool in writing a new canon on Blackness and disability. In light of the fact that early Christian literature demonstrates the power of religious rhetoric to create categories of bodies, it is important to note that the use of the Christian religion to create categories of health, beauty, and desire have also shaped Western medicine. The creation of "damned" bodies is the creation of undesirable bodies, and the politics of desire places White, male, and abled bodies as the central measuring point for determining which bodies can gain access to the status of normal and beautiful.

There are new orators on the horizon who are both challenging destructive definitions of Blackness, disability, and health and changing the terms used to define which bodies are best. These new voices are historians of Christian literature like Kristin Kobes Du Mez, whose book *Jesus and John Wayne* exposes the history of the American "warrior" version of Jesus, whose perfect body is built for conquest and domination, or disabled Christian theologians like Amy Kenny, whose book *My Body Is Not a Prayer Request* advocates for religious reform in the area of disability, health, and body imagery.

Another critical work is *The 1619 Project*, created by Nikole Hannah-Jones. Hannah-Jones is a journalist and investigative reporter focusing on racial injustice. She is a correspondent for the *New York Times Magazine* and a 2020 Pulitzer Prize winner (for The 1619 Project). The project and its related book reframe American history by placing slavery at the center of its narrative. In chapter 12 of *The 1619 Project*, the author speaks of a Black woman, Susan Moore, who had contracted COVID-19 and was hospitalized, only to die two weeks later, after doctors failed to provide her proper medical aid. Moore, a physician, made a video with her mobile phone recording her frustrations with the lack of concern or care her doctors showed. She says, "He made me feel like I was a drug addict. And he knew I was a physician. I don't take narcotics. I was hurting." Moore goes on to say, "I put forth and I maintain if I was white, I wouldn't have to go through that. This is how Black people get killed."[20]

Black (and disabled) people are being killed, and they are being killed because religion in America has made it possible to see the medical issues of minority bodies as moral issues, issues of their character, issues of their lack of discipline. Most importantly, it has made it both possible and acceptable to see their preexisting conditions or comorbidities as caused by their body or their race rather than formed out of our ableist and racist history, which has shaped bias against dark-skinned and disabled bodies. Yet with the rise of new voices, a new canon is being created. What was once the accepted narrative about Black bodies is slowly being exposed as a work of fiction.

Blackballed

Ableism and the Black Church

I remember the first time I realized I was Black. Of course, I was fully aware of the color of my skin, but being Black isn't simply about having dark skin. We know race is a social construct, and yet we seldom realize the weight of what this means.

I remember my discovery vividly, as it came about due to being surprised that the world was not just Black and White. Without exaggeration, I can honestly say that until around the age of ten or eleven years old, I did not know that there were more than two races or ethnicities. In my young mind, either a person was Black or a person was White, and Whiteness was the absolute antithesis of Blackness. White people were White because I was Black, and to be completely honest, I felt no type of ambivalence about my designation as a Black person until I understood that the world was not solely Black and White.

My father served in the Army for well over two decades. Our family lived overseas. Most of my memories were of living in Germany and visiting other European countries while he was doing a three-year tour of duty. I'm not quite certain why it never occurred to me that the world was full of different cultures, ethnicities, and races, when I spent at least a third of my elementary school life living in a different country. Perhaps my distorted view of the world resulted from living in the binary racial milieu of South Georgia prior to that. My earliest memories of going to school in Georgia led my young, impressionable mind to believe that the world was Black and White, and there were always, always far more White people than there were Black, and the numbers determined which group mattered most.

When we returned from our tour in Germany, my father accepted his next post at Fort Bliss in El Paso, Texas. The first day we arrived in the city, it was a sweltering 114 degrees. This was going to be a challenge for me. I wasn't wrong, but it wasn't because of the scorching heat. My exposure to my ignorance about race and ethnicity was blistering. It was February, Black History Month, and like most elementary schools, my peers and I were engaged in learning about the history of Black people in America. We had the typical lessons about the heroes of the civil rights movement, such as Martin Luther King Jr. and Rosa Parks and their contemporaries. We also learned about some of the other well-known figures in Black history, like Harriet Tubman.

What made the day a defining moment in my young life occurred after our obligatory discussion about the treatment of African Americans before and during the civil rights movement. It has always been a point of contention for me that American history always begins the story about Black bodies by relegating them to slaves brought into the Western world. But on this occasion, it proved to be a pivotal conversation. During the lunch period, I sat at the table with a classmate who spent most of his time lamenting the awful treatment of Black people by White slave owners and opponents of civil rights. While I appreciated his empathy, his tone (and words) distanced himself from those atrocities. His exact words were "I'm really sorry about what they did to your people."

Until that moment, I hadn't quite processed the entire Black history discussion as a "my people" and "their people" binary, especially as it related to my White classmates being lumped into the category of "their" people. The thought simply hadn't crossed my mind until my classmate presented the discussion as a very binary relationship between Black people and White people. Perhaps this is where unconscious bias emerges. At least in the moment, mine did.

Reducing the discussion of race relations to "us" versus "them" seemed to poke at the parts of me where my ignorance about racism (and ableism) lived. It is the dark place in most of us that finds comfort in defending our right to exist by choosing a stance that protects us from being attached to a horrific history. Deep down, the vast majority of those of us who live in the shadow of such sin long to rid ourselves of the residue that slavery has left behind. And still, we can't quite achieve this goal without relinquishing our allegiance to our West-washed view of the world, of people of color, and of people with disabilities. We are all— Black and White, disabled and able-bodied—victims of the results of slavery. Like Micah in the book of Judges, we are shaped by the results of the initial sin. Its wickedness has long had its way with us.

I believe that is why my response to my classmate was sharp and defensive. "What do you mean 'they'?" I said. "Don't you mean you're sorry about what 'we' did to your people?"

"Well," my classmate responded, "I'm actually Hispanic, not White." My first thought was that he was making this up. It's a ridiculous assumption, I know, but I was eleven and, until that time, had no clue what he was talking about. Even after traveling the world at a very young age, I had no clue what a Hispanic person was. In my young, ignorant mind, people were Black or White. Eleven years and several countries and languages into my then very short life, I learned that the world is a place full of various races, ethnicities, and cultures and that my identity as a young, Black male was not a default based on the only other race that existed on earth. To say that I was embarrassed is a colossal understatement.

For far too long, the false binary of Black and White shaped my perception of the world. I suppose this was due to my personal lack of exposure to worldviews that challenged both ableism and racism. For many of us, whether we are aware of it or not, the world is largely defined by ableist and racist ideology, even if we don't personally subscribe to those ideas. Ableism centers the experience of certain bodies, bodies that are considered best, and the rest of the world finds their place in relation to how closely they can position themselves to what is normal, right, and preferred. What usually results is a sense of otherness that extends far beyond a realization that one is different. That includes a feeling of being cast into a liminal space, a void where the voiceless wander, worry, and wonder how to assert a sense of self that isn't reduced to an inability to present itself as a White body.

That's why the Black church is so important in the discussion of ableism and racism. For centuries, the historically Black church and her sister institutions have provided a sanctuary for bodies and bodies of work that were deemed deficient or abnormal. In this chapter, I want to explore the role that the Black church has played in the evolution of human and civil rights in this nation, the benefits of the Black church's influence on disability rights, and how the Black church must advance its own commitment to anti-ableism as part of its ongoing justice motif.

The Beginning of the Black Church

Over the course of two decades, I have been in pastoral ministry. I've been blessed to serve in a wide variety of roles, from young adult and youth pastorates, serving at a private Christian school, to hospice chaplaincy and lead pastorates of three different churches. I've also had the privilege of planting a church that I pastored for four years. Every church that I have led, including the church that I currently lead, has been multiethnic. When I say "multiethnic," I mean a church composed of people representing more than two races. Although most multiracial churches are doing great work, there is often a sense in which the overall presentation of the church—in its leadership, culture, music, and ministry approach—leans away from the cultural influences of minorities. This includes persons with disabilities. A multiethnic church attempts to move past diversity for diversity's sake and to actively and intentionally incorporate the nonmajority culture into the church. The music, the leadership, the ministry model, and the programs are all constantly trying to reflect the value the church has for all people, and among the many minority influences is the influence of the Black church.

Years ago, I was attending a monthly church-leadership lunch for those interested in doing multicultural and multiethnic ministry. The groups usually were well attended, with a core number of people who came regularly and many new faces each month. The goal of the groups was to facilitate relationships between pastors and church leaders that would hopefully improve race relations. These groups launched a few years prior to the national backlash following the murders of George Floyd and Ahmaud Arbery, so they didn't form in response to those defining moments in American culture. Yet they did see an increase in interest and attendance following those events. They also experienced an increase in intensity.

One day, the subject of our meeting shifted to the need for multiethnic leadership when building a truly diverse congregation. As the discussion progressed, someone noted that most mainline multiethnic churches are led by White pastors. They asked why we thought this was the case. One pastor, a White pastor of a prominent multiethnic church, spoke up and said he believed it was because many White

Christians still have difficulty following a Black leader. The discussion then took a turn. I'll spare you the details of the heated debate and fast-forward to the prominent point of rebuttal made by several pastors at the meeting. After all the platitudes, they shared that the perceived reason why many White Christians find it difficult to follow Black leaders or to attend historically Black churches is that there is a perceived difference in the quality of teaching and doctrine associated with the Black church and Black pastoral leadership.

That perceived difference was a perceived *deficiency*. After pressing for a more substantive description of what was meant by "different," we discovered that many of the pastors attending were defending the lack of White attendance at historically Black churches. It was because they honestly believed, based on their pastoral experience, that the Black church didn't pass most White Christians' test of orthodoxy. Not willingly attending a historically Black church was not a matter of diversity for them but a matter of doctrine. To be clear, not all the White pastors at the meeting agreed with this; rather, some were simply voicing the sentiment that many people would never actually admit to about why they would struggle to attend a historically Black church or even a multiethnic church in which the pastor was Black.

In 2019, around the same time as the pastors meeting, a 2016 video of prominent White evangelical pastor James White resurfaced. According to his ministry website, White is the director of Alpha and Omega Ministries. He is a pastor and elder at a church in Arizona and a professor of church history and apologetics. In a July 2016 clip of his show called "The Dividing Line," White discusses several topics, including the "woke church," critical theory, and identity politics.[1] During that broadcast, White makes the following statement: "What struck me was there is in a sense—oh boy am I gonna get in trouble for this—in many churches of whatever ethnic mix, there is an anti-intellectualism, an anti-church history-ism, there is an anti-theology-ism, there is an anti-Bible translation, Bible transmission-ism, and it's seen in the fact that it's almost never addressed . . . , but it's especially true in black churches. It's just the reality. The idea of sound doctrine, church history, there are so few."[2]

I was raised in the Black church. The Black church has shaped me in profound ways, but it has had no greater influence on my life than in its commitment to creative, imaginative, and prophetic justice-oriented preaching. The Black church has long been an incubator for some of the greatest religious and secular leaders in American history, yet still—in what is supposed to be a postracial America—many agree with White regarding the historically Black church. They believe that the Black church is inferior.

Here is the startling truth about sentiments like White's. What presents itself as an issue of doctrine is really at its core an issue of disability discrimination. Racial bias plays a role in views regarding the inferiority of the Black church. The ultimate culprit in such views is ableism. Ableism is the ideology that gives birth to notions of physical (and mental) inferiority. What White and others say about the Black church exemplifies the brand of Christianity that was crafted to ensure the enslavement of Africans. Black bodies and minds were thought to be inherently inferior to their White counterparts. As a result, they were effectively disabled and incapable of living up to the intellectual, emotional, spiritual, and religious standards of their owners. This idea is nothing new, yet the residue of ableism is still clinging to the very notion that Black spirituality is deficient because it comes from Black bodies and minds.

This idea is demonstrated in how Europeans disregarded African traditional religions. Such disregard was much less about comparing these religions to the merits of Christianity than it was about asserting that African peoples were ahistorical, meaning they had no history considered adequate enough to deem them a civilized people. In European minds, this was especially true of African spiritual practices.

The irony of believing that the Black church, Black preaching, and Black theology are inferior is that *Black people didn't invent the Black church.* In the earliest days of colonial settlement, all churches were multiracial. While enslaved Africans often held secret church services after hours, they also could gather for Christian worship provided that a White person supervised the services to monitor what was being taught. Despite these gatherings, the church in America was organized and led by Whites, especially in the South. In the early 1800s, because of the Second Great Awakening, the number of Africans joining the Baptist and Methodist traditions skyrocketed.

The Methodist Church openly opposed slavery, at least as an institution, which made it appealing to many Africans. Richard Allen (1760–1831), a former slave who had worked to purchase his freedom, joined St. George's Methodist Episcopal Church in Philadelphia. He soon became a popular pastor, preaching about the struggle for freedom and liberation among Blacks. Allen, among many other

Black preachers, was often included in the worship experiences of White-led churches, although he and his fellow Black pastors constantly battled against discrimination and paternalism. In 1792, racial tensions came to a boil when Absalom Jones (1746–1818), an associate of Allen's, was instructed to leave the White section of the church and proceed to the "nigger pews."[3]

As a result, Allen and Jones exited the Methodist Church; scores of Black attendees exited with them in solidarity. The Black church, representing various denominations, including the African Methodist Episcopal Church, emerged as a response to the rejection of Black bodies sharing space with White congregants. The Black church did not grow as a parallel to the White church; it grew as a *protest* to White Christians' theology, which deemed it unnecessary and unsafe to practice their faith with Black Christians. At its origin, the historically Black church stood as a response to readings of the biblical text that erroneously allowed for the subjugation of Black bodies that were defined as disabled or deficient.

The Blessing of the Black Church

Despite the ableist and racist roots of the Black church's beginning, the historically Black church has been a tremendous blessing to Western Christianity. Both the teachings and the traditions born out of the Black church have influenced some of the nation's greatest movements toward justice, equality, and equity in the twenty-first century. The Black church has also been the primary incubator for courageous spiritual and religious leaders of the past. The enduring impact of national leaders like Martin Luther King Jr. is evidence of the Black church's power and relevance. Out of the hallowed halls of the Black church have emerged both a message and messengers that have provided the West with an alternative interpretation of the God of the biblical text. In the Black church, the God of the text is a God of justice, a God who sides with the oppressed, and a God who calls his people to work toward the liberation of all.

The Black church was the primary instigator of a way of reading the biblical text that challenged slavery and Jim Crow laws. The Black church rarely gets the credit it deserves for its rich history of biblical interpretation. We should temper comments from pastors and scholars like James White about the legitimacy and value of the Black church, considering that the Black church's creation resulted from an assumption that to be Black is to be disabled and inherently and eternally inferior. What White and others cannot admit is that they did not design the doctrine and theology that has proceeded from the historically Black church to accommodate the same ableist and racist theology that created it. Black theology became necessary because Western Christianity all but removed Black and disabled bodies from the story of God's grace and redemption. Justice was hardly a focus, and equality and equity were not attributes of the God of the colonizers.

The Black church has brought along a far more robust and accurate reading of the text, one that does not omit portions of Scripture alluding to equality in God's eyes, but one that centers the experience and expression of God as those of a God who turns an ear to the slave and the oppressed and responds by exercising holy judgment and heavenly justice in a world that is broken and biased. The Black church has functioned like the prophets of the Old Testament did. Cloaked in the tradition of Isaiah, Ezekiel, Amos, and Micah, the Black church has heralded a call to national holiness, a holiness that stretches beyond the boundaries of worn-down wooden pews and spills out into the streets that have long been riddled with Black and disabled bodies. The Black church has long been the prophetic voice that has spoken against the building of a nation and a religion by willingly and intentionally sacrificing non-White, disabled bodies for the sake of religious imperialism.

One of the most important contributions of the historically Black church is its provision of a safe space for bodies excluded from the mainstream church. According to Henry Louis Gates, a prominent scholar and African American historian, "Black houses of worship would shelter a nation within a nation, gradually becoming the political and spiritual centers of local Black communities."[4] The Black church is a model for creating antiableist spaces that can challenge societal misconceptions about both Blackness and disability.

In the following chapters, we will look at the ways in which the Black church has contributed to a change in the material conditions of Black people, particularly in the South. The Black church viewed its involvement in the civil rights movement as a matter of Christian conviction, a conviction that repudiated the Christianity that created the ableist and racist caste system in America. We'll look more closely at some methods that the Black church has employed in its pursuit of justice and the impact that it can have on furthering the justice movement for the disability community.

The Black church can play an essential role in dismantling both ableism and racism in American Christianity, and yet there are a few ways in which the Black church must first address its complicity in the ableist ideology that gave birth to its existence.

Bettering the Black Church Experience (and Witness)

The historically Black church is perhaps the best example of an institution that has had a positive influence on impacting systematic injustices. It provides us with a model of institutionally prophetic ministry, a ministry that mobilizes the marginalized and gives voice to their experience of God. We should consider the Black church one of the greatest available resources in dismantling ableist and racist theology and doctrine. Yet the church, like many other marginalized groups, has struggled with the internalization of the very standards that excluded it from the mainstream.

Over the last several years, I have taken part in and helped plan a number of disability ministry conferences. I have been able to share with congregations across the country about disability inclusion. One of the most striking observations that I have had in the last ten years pertains to the lack of diversity in these conferences. Most of the conference speakers and conference attendees are White. Engaging Black churches on disability has been one of the most persistent struggles of doing disability ministry.

To be clear, the historically Black church is not an institution opposed to including the disabled. The Black community has a history of its own practice of disability inclusion, but because of the impact of slavery, ministry to and with disabled persons in the Black church is often an invisible institution. This is to say, you most likely won't find a formalized or structured ministry for persons with disabilities in many Black churches, but this doesn't mean that those congregants aren't cared for, loved, and accepted. Many of these parishioners do not attend church in a physical location for a variety of reasons; nevertheless, there is often an informal system of church support and pastoral care that is regularly extended to these people. It is not uncommon for the average attender to be unaware that such services are even being provided to at-home members.

Disability ministry in the Black church context is often invisible because it stems from the days of slavery and the need to shelter those with disabilities from harm or violence. Slave owners saw Black bodies that were physically (or mentally) disabled as a monetary liability. They did not see them as people but as bodies born and bred to produce labor. If a person they saw as property became unable to meet the rigorous and debilitating physical demands placed on their bodies, they faced the possibility of death. This was true even though a large percentage of physical disabilities among enslaved Africans were due to harsh conditions and torture.

When a child was born with a physical disability, communities would often conspire to lie to slave owners by telling them that the child did not survive birth in order to shield them from terrible forms of treatment, including being drowned so that slave owners would not have to feed and clothe someone who would not give them a sufficient return in the form of labor. What emerged because of this need to protect the disabled is what I call the "shadowing" of the disability community. We often see shadowing in the Black church and the Black community in the various ways that they shield the disabled from the harsh treatment of an ableist society. Many Black churches have informal disability ministries, ministries that provide support to the disabled without placing a spotlight on the ministry and, subsequently, the people they are serving and their families.

The downside to these shadow services is that they often isolate families by shielding them from other services or resources that may be of benefit to them. As a Black man diagnosed as autistic fairly late in life, I know well the challenge of growing up without additional resources that could have been beneficial for me during my development. The Black community readily recognizes the discrimination it faces because of racism, and it attempts to erase the impact of ableism by not openly addressing disability—at the cost of missing out on needed support from outside the Black community. Access to diagnostic services and treatment continues to be an ongoing challenge in the Black community, and ableism and racism play a prominent role in the disparities.

While the Black church has been an incubator for spiritual leadership and scholarship in the areas of justice and equality, the Black church, as an institution, has not been completely immune to internalized ableism. It is important to note that Black churches are not a monolith, yet the Black church has struggled with internalized ableism in how it has historically handled issues of gender and sexuality. The intention of this book is not to explore those issues but to acknowledge that while the Black church has much to discuss in dismantling ableism, it is not without its own need to progress in some areas. As an institution born out of ableist and exclusionary origins, the Black church continues to develop its prophetic voice for justice.

The Disabled God and
the Rise of the American Jesus

So when he returned the money to his mother, she took
200 silver coins and gave them to a silversmith, who made
them into an image and an idol. And these were placed in
Micah's house.

—Judges 17:4

The story of Micah and his mother reminds us that humans crave idols. We all, from time to time, need a tangible placeholder for all our hopes and dreams. Ideals such as faith, love, hope, courage, and even God encourage us to ascend to the heights of the human experience, and yet, without something tangible, something to touch, or sometimes someone to talk to or about, those abstract ideals lose their luster. I am not convinced that having images to look to for inspiration is unholy. We need images to inspire us. We need something or someone to represent who we believe we can become.

I grew up loving sports. I played many of them. Soccer. Basketball. I even had a very brief boxing career, which served to help me discover that I don't enjoy getting punched in the face. Out of all the sports I played, football was the one I loved the most. I always dreamed of making it big. Playing in the NFL was every young football fan's dream. Spoiler alert: I fell woefully short of achieving that dream, but I did play at a small private college in Wisconsin called Concordia University.

When my plans for making it to the NFL didn't pan out, I moved to Atlanta after graduation, married my wife, and began my life with her. My first job out of college was in retail-loss prevention. Within six months, I became a manager at a local store, and along with management came some pretty cool perks for a twenty-two-year-old recent college graduate. No perk was cooler than the two days I would spend with my all-time-favorite football idol, the recently retired Jerry Rice. Rice is the greatest wide receiver to ever play the game. He is in the NFL Hall of Fame and holds several records to this day. He had recently retired and had released a line of chewable vitamins in the nationwide retail chain I worked for, and for two consecutive days, my colleagues and I provided security for Rice as he did in-store appearances in the Atlanta area market.

Jerry Rice was a really nice guy. Very personable. We even played a little pretend one-on-one basketball in the store's break room. At the end of the two days, he signed a football for me. My football career was just as over as his was, and yet those two days did something for me. Rice didn't come from one of the most prestigious universities. He played at a historically Black university called Mississippi Valley State. You may have never even heard of it. He wasn't even the fastest when compared to other wide receivers of his era. What Jerry Rice was, though, was a hard worker and someone who was driven to be the best. I suppose that's why he was still my idol.

Idols matter because they give us images that we can relate to. When God gives instructions to Moses about how to structure life after the exodus, he urges the formerly enslaved Israelites to make him the ultimate priority. The rule about not having any other gods before the true and living God is God's acknowledgment that in life, we will have relationships with people and with ideals that will constantly compete with our relationship with God. God wants to be the priority over those people and ideals, those images, and those idols we hold on to. That's why God frowns upon his people when they create graven images. We face the same challenge that Micah faced. More often than not, we create images and idols that are born out of our desperate desire to unseat God as the number one priority.

Disability theology, starting mainly with theologian Nancy Eiesland, begins by unseating many of the images and idols we hold dear. Ableism doesn't merely deny disabled people their rights; ableism also rejects the disabled symbols and imagery. Representation matters. It matters even more in religion because religion is so abstract that we need images and symbols to help us grasp an invisible God. The Old and New Testaments are replete with symbols and images used to convey messages from and messages about the God of Israel. From stone tablets to tents, tabernacles, and temples, images and symbols help us relate to God. But when our images and symbols of God merely reflect rather than upend our sinful discrimination against people with disabilities, we know we've created an idol that harms.

The late doctor Nancy Eiesland wrote a book that helps us understand the importance of disabled people having religious images and symbols that they can identify with. *The Disabled God: Toward a Liberatory Theology of Disability* was published by Abingdon Press in 1994. Eiesland was born with a congenital bone defect that caused her to undergo several corrective surgeries as a child. She would live with chronic pain and disability until her death at the age of forty-four. Eiesland was a pioneer in disability theology, and her work has influenced scores of theologians and authors also engaging in the work of disability theology and disability justice.

Chapter 4 of Eiesland's book bears the same title as that of her book, and it serves as an entry point into the conversation about disability theology. There, Eiesland contends that God is disabled (this view will be addressed in the next section, under the heading "Theological Implications of a Disabled God"). She presents a concept of God that includes the lived experience of disabled people. Like many theologies rooted in liberation, disability theology begins with the experience of a marginalized group and explores the need for that group to envision God in ways that speak to their unique experience.

Disability theology relies heavily on respecting embodied experiences. In this way, the Christian doctrine of the incarnation suggests that God communicates with humanity in ways that are accessible to our bodies, no matter how those bodies function. The incarnation tells us that bodies have a central role in the practice of faith.

Embracing embodiment means that the particularities of our bodies profoundly shape how we receive and respond to religious experiences. Feminist and womanist theologians have called attention to this reality by centering gender, race, and ethnicity as important parts of the human experience. In doing so, they have helped to move the discussion of theology toward a more contextualized view of religious experiences. After all, if the human experience is one of having a body, then different body types must be considered. If body types matter in the discussion of theology, then persons with disabilities need to have a theology that pays attention to their bodies.

Eiesland also believes that the practice of religion should be connected with the ability to inform and influence social status, which means religious symbols are important. Religious symbols are powerful conduits and connectors between the abstract, immaterial, invisible, and often mysterious world of faith and religion, on the one hand, and the material and practical expression of the human and divine relationship, on the other. Symbols are important tools for religious expression, and yet there must be symbols that connect to the religious experiences of different bodies.

Symbols are important because disabled bodies also need representation in their religious experiences. Because religion is often deeply rooted in symbols and imagery of wholeness, disability theology recognizes the need for symbols and imagery that reimagine wholeness in ways that represent persons with varying degrees of disability and religious expression. These symbols are needed not just to provide meaning for those with disabilities within the Christian community; they are also needed to relate to and provide meaning for able-bodied people who share a faith in Jesus. By providing disability-inclusive religious symbols for both disabled and able-bodied followers of Jesus, the role of stigma, which often manifests in either an aversion to or an inappropriate fascination with disabled bodies, dissipates.

Political action is a vital part of disability theology's method. Central to political action is the need for centering the voices and experiences of the disabled. Only by doing so can we all challenge and dismantle ableist ideologies that wrongly suggest God is able-bodied, White, and male. This requires those who are able-bodied to share space with and live in proximity to the disability community. Increased visibility and increased influence are two of the many ways we can achieve this goal.

Proximity paves the road to liberation because the very presence of disabled bodies serves as a visible protest to societal structures that place disabled people at the lowest rung of the social ladder. According to Eiesland, "'Acting out' means refusing to acquiesce to the acceptable role for people with disabilities: it is the revolutionary work of resistance."[1] Disability theology seeks to serve as the primary source of hope for a community of overly marginalized people both in society and in the social order of the Western church. And yet, for Eiesland, there is the stark reality that resistance, revolution, even rebellion, if you will, requires much from the bodies of those who want to take part in acts of liberation. The work of liberation is a labor that often tests the mental, emotional, and physical energy of the liberator. This is a haunting reality for persons living with disabilities. The work is very often not physically easy to do.

Political action also means attending to the reality of the types and amounts of energy that are needed to embark on this work. It means being willing to place one's body on the line for the sake of liberation, while acknowledging the existing fatigue that accompanies life with a disability. Eiesland is careful to navigate this tension, and yet she believes that health, well-being, and survival are at the core of all spiritual practices aimed at liberation. This displaces the notion of virtuous suffering—the idea that physical suffering is good and blessed and should be gladly welcomed. If we consider this, we must pay particular attention to the accep tance of one's body as it is, even in the face of limitations.

The acceptance of bodies is a key part of the liberatory work of disability theology, especially because society has become obsessed with the denial of limitations. In a world where disabled people are taught to loathe their bodies, accepting and celebrating disabled bodies is an act of public protest. This radical acceptance of disability and of disabled bodies as an act of resistance is best done not in isolation but in union with both other bodies within the disability community and other marginalized people groups. The union between people with disabilities and other marginalized people groups also calls for an unrelenting resistance to societal pressure to rank degrees of disability and discrimination. Solidarity in resistance is also solidarity in acceptance and appreciation for all bodies that find themselves victims of a system of oppression. According to Eiesland, this includes people of color, women, and the poor.

This is where Black theology and disability theology complement each other. Both anchor their ideas about God and about faith in the life-giving hope that the God of the Bible is a God who is for the marginalized. Black theology and disability theology lean heavily on this hope for their respective communities. God is a God of liberation. God is a God of justice.

Over the past several years, we have witnessed varying factions of American Christianity debate and disagree about the role of justice in the life of the Christian. We saw it once again in the spring of 2020, shortly after the beginning of the global pandemic. Just a few weeks into the global shutdown, the pandemic forced us to slow down the busy pace of our lives. It was during this time of adjustment to a new way of living that a spotlight was shined on an incidence of racial violence. Scores of well-meaning people were exposed to just a modicum of the reality that so many people of color face. The catalyst for this confrontation was the murder of George Floyd.

The death of Floyd brought to light once again that justice and equality are still not realities for many bodies of color. With the viral exposure of Floyd's death on camera came an exposure to the culture wars within American Christianity that have always existed, yet the tensions seemed to be much thicker following Floyd's death. Many communities of color, including communities of faith, called out for justice. The call for justice is a common cry in marginalized communities. It is a recurring refrain for people of color and for those with disabilities. Like many people of color, persons with disabilities, and other minorities who practice Christianity, I believe that justice for many marginalized communities should be the preeminent concern of both Christianity and our culture.

Disability theology, much like liberation theology, shines the spotlight on the social conditions of people on the lowest rung of the caste system. For disability theologians, justice is meant to intertwine with the social norms and social conditions of the most oppressed among us. In fact, disability theologians believe that justice is one of the main goals of God's agenda in creating a people to call his own.

In Genesis 18:19, we read that God purposefully chooses Abraham, the father of the Jewish faith, so that he would "direct his sons and their families to keep the way of the LORD by doing what is right and just." The prophet Micah also instructs the people of Israel to focus on God's goal of justice, saying, "He has told you, O mortal, what is good, and what does the Lord require of you but to do justice and to love kindness and to walk humbly with your God?" (Mic. 6:8 NRSVue). In this verse alone, we can reasonably conclude that justice is always social. One thing is certain when it comes to the Christian faith and heritage: the God of injustice does not exist.

Despite the fact that the Bible portrays the God of Israel as the God of justice, the God who sides with the marginalized and the oppressed, Western versions of Christianity developed by determining that the gospel of Jesus and the God of justice had no power to bring liberation to slaves in America. This was an intentional move by colonial slaveholders, who used disability as their primary tool to devalue and justify control over them. In making Black bodies exempt from the complete impact of the gospel, we see the evil of ableism operating within the confines of Christianity in the West. By adjusting the faith to meet the economic goals of slavery, the colonists effectively changed the Jesus narrative to perpetuate injustice and inequality. Black bodies were said to be inherently inferior, and it is here that we see the religious use of ableism being used to prop up racial bias in America.

This is why mainstream evangelical theology needs to engage with both Black liberation theology and disability theology. In order to reverse engineer the effects of ableism and its subsequent impact on racism in America, we have to engage a theology that unravels harmful images of Black bodies, especially images that present them as inherently disabled. This is important for two reasons. First, any theology that presents disabled people as inferior and incapable of fully reflecting God's image is in fact ableist. Second, any theology that uses disability as a tool to displace and marginalize an entire group of people based on the color of their skin is both ableist and racist, and that theology is incapable of self-correction. Engaging with disability theology and its push to provide positive images of a God who identifies with and works in and through the disabled is how we pave a path forward, away from ableism. When Eiesland contends that God is disabled, she is providing a way forward for the church.

Theological Implications of a Disabled God

Central to a theology of disability is the idea that God is disabled. This concept derives from stories of the postresurrection Jesus still bearing the marks of his torture and execution, specifically the wounds or holes in his hands

110

and in his side. Eiesland writes, "In the resurrected Jesus Christ, [the disciples] saw not the suffering servant for whom the last and most important word was tragedy and sin, but the disabled God who embodied both impaired hands and feet and pierced side and the imago Dei."[2] Eiesland's ideas about the disabled body of the postresurrection Jesus are rooted in her reading of the Gospel writer Luke's recording of his return. "While they were talking about this, Jesus himself stood among them and said to them, 'Peace be with you.' They were startled and terrified and thought that they were seeing a ghost. He said to them, 'Why are you frightened, and why do doubts arise in your hearts? Look at my hands and my feet, see that it is I myself. Touch me and see, for a ghost does not have flesh and bones as you see that I have'" (Luke 24:36–39 NRSVue).

An important aspect of disability theology is the acknowledgment of the need to contextualize Christology. This is why the image of Jesus as the disabled God is critical in addressing both ableism and racism. In Jesus, the disabled God, we are introduced to a God whose incarnation places him into the exact situation that despised bodies find themselves in. This image challenges the ways in which able-bodiedness (or Whiteness) has historically served as the center of theological inquiry. Contextualization is the placement of the history of Jesus as a person and as a religious symbol into conversation with the present and with the present condition of those who encounter this history. By stepping into history, we observe and study and understand God (to a degree), so the Christian doctrine of the incarnation is the epitome of contextualization.

God uses the human body, and what God does with that body is of utmost importance for understanding God's intimate connection to human experience. The postresurrection Jesus becomes the gateway for understanding the *imago Dei* in the Christian tradition. Jesus, God embodied, returns to life, and he remains impaired by choice, despite miraculously transcending the physical realities of human death. It is important to note that God, in this act, uses transcendence to become more tangible. The best and most accurate way to interpret the intentions of God and the image of God in all of humanity is to gaze upon the disabled God, an image of God that holds within it the tension between the divine perfection and the realities of human frailty.

Eiesland's work helps us grasp the theological implications of a disabled God. The postresurrection body of Jesus, one that retains disability and willingly occupies the status of the despised body, has enormous power for transforming the social body hierarchy. The image of a holy God choosing to eternally inhabit a despised body places the power of the resurrection story not at the center of the worship of the normal but at the margin. The place of the disabled. The place of the despised. The place of the disregarded.

This image of God helps those with disabilities and those who care for them to engage in a christological conversation about the need for a closer examination of the postresurrection body of Jesus. This image is also critically important in understanding the Black body in society. In early American Christianity, the despised and disregarded body was the Black body of enslaved Africans. Their designation as inherently disabled put their bodies at the bottom rung of the body hierarchy.

The postresurrection body of Jesus—not the White, Western, sanitized version but the one we read about in Scripture—tells us that God in Christ knows what it means to live with impairment, immortality, and most importantly, dignity for despised bodies. In the postresurrection Jesus, God uses his spiritual authority and power to reverse death while *retaining* disability. Jesus allows his physical body to remain intimately connected with a body that would have been despised. This raises the question: How is the church engaging in an interpretation of God's intentions and character based on what God (Jesus) does with his body?

God's message is found in his methods. Seeing Jesus as the disabled God changes the questions that we ask of God and of God's message to humanity, not just in his route to death but in his stunning reversal of death. Jesus, the disabled God, is not just a God with a supernatural ability who uses that power to avoid or reverse uncomfortable and often deadly forms of discrimination against his body. Jesus, the disabled God, presents those results of the discrimination against his person as the primary point of his postresurrection identification. This image is hope not only to the disabled but to the Black bodies who have been believed to be disabled and inferior. In Jesus, we see the radical reorienting of the body hierarchy. Disability is no longer a despised state of humanity but a place of dignity and glory.

The postresurrection Jesus invites humanity to identify him, by his choice, not only as the savior of the world but as a God who also survives the world. His marks, the wounds that remain, can serve as a new symbol communicating that physical impairment or disability is not abhorrent to God—either in history or in eternity—nor does faith in him require a complete and total erasure of certain aspects of our human experience, including disability and Blackness. The disabled God is a new and liberating symbol of God's acknowledgment and acceptance of the human experience and the limits of humanity as a foundational part of what brings integrity to his desire for an intimate and eternal relationship with creation. For the disability community, the disabled God is a symbol not only of hope but of dignity and ultimately of justice for those who so desperately need it. And for the Black community, the disabled God is a restorative symbol of dignity, which was once stripped from the community's identity by placing the label of "disabled" upon their dark skin. Jesus, the disabled God, is a symbol of life and liberation for all bodies that dwell at the bottom of the body hierarchy. His body becomes our proof that God's image is radiantly shining through what was once despised and disregarded. So why don't we often encounter this version of Jesus in Western theology? How did we end up with an image of Jesus that distances him from despised bodies?

Two Models of Disability

In order to understand the rise of the American Jesus, we have to understand the two basic views or models of disability. First, there is the medical model of disability, and second, there is the social model. The medical model of disability focuses primarily on causes and cures. It is rooted in a biomedical understanding of health, which considers health in terms of biological factors alone. This model aims to produce research that can uncover the root cause of an impairment. It perceives disability to be a challenge that is a

114

condition based on a person's body, its inability to function properly, and the direct cause of the condition.

The medical model of disability emphasizes curative measures rather than community support. If the source of a disability is disease, physical or mental trauma, or other underlying health conditions, then the goal is a cure or, at least, the provision of sufficient and sustainable medical care to give the disabled person the most normal life possible.

The social model of disability departs significantly from the medical model. While the medical model focuses on the individual with the disability and curative measures, the social model pays acute attention to society and how it categorizes persons with disabilities. This model views disability not as an impairment to be managed by an individual through medical intervention, but as a more complex phenomenon related to how *certain narratives about disability are more disabling than the biological impairment.* In this model, disability exists largely because of environments that don't accommodate a disabled person's physical, emotional, and psychological needs. The social model advocates for ridding society of structures that serve as barriers for the disabled.

A Westernized version of Jesus has replaced the Jesus of the Gospels, the Jesus with holes in his wrists and in his side. I believe that the reason mainstream evangelical theology rejects the disabled God is because Western Christianity is inherently ableist. Our world is profoundly shaped by the medical model of disability, a model that promotes the view that "abnormal" bodies are deficient and need to be fixed. We have done this to Jesus. In fact, I believe we are so ableist that we even discriminate against God.

Even in its best expressions, Western Christianity is at least guilty of trying to heal the disabling marks that identify the postresurrection Jesus to his earliest followers and to us. We taint our version of Christianity with ableist notions that will not allow us to serve a disabled savior. Like many disabled people who are trapped beneath the weight of a model of disability that views their bodies as burdens to be fixed and healed, Jesus also finds himself the victim of ableist ideology because we have reduced his disability to wounds—wounds that are described as something akin to childhood scars that remain after falling off a bike or scraping a knee while playing soccer in the street. The American Jesus is not disabled because we have taken the initiative to help him ascend to body normativity. But Jesus never asks us to fix him. He simply asks for our faith. He asks us to place our faith in his body, which has returned from the grave with disability and has confirmed that he eternally intertwined his divinity with his human experience.

The holes in Jesus's hands have been filled with Western ideals. Until fairly recently, we accepted images of Jesus as a White man with blond hair and blue eyes. From portraits hanging over the baptismal to the back of the handheld fans we used to cool ourselves in our sweltering sanctuaries in the summer, even to the inside cover of the large family Bible that lies reverently on the coffee table, we transformed Jesus into the ideal body, and he looked nothing like the images described in the Bible. While we have been diligent over the last few decades to unravel some of the unhealthy images that we created of Jesus, we have a long way to go. The Western Jesus no longer bears the marks of disability because the American Jesus is a winner. The American

Jesus is a warrior. The American Jesus is aggressive and "appropriately" violent. (I mean, he did flip over tables in the temple, right?) The American Jesus cannot have holes in his hands and a large hole in his side because the body of the Jesus we want has to represent the type of Christians we want to be—while conveniently setting aside the commands related to loving our enemies, praying for those who persecute us, and turning the other cheek. The Jesus who said those things, we surmise, is weak and naive.

The enemy-loving Jesus, the Jesus of justice and mercy and grace, isn't exactly the Jesus who would endorse mass genocide, racial slavery, discrimination against disabled people, or the violence and vitriol that sometimes occurs in Christian communities. So we healed him. We changed his body into a body we could get behind. A body without disability. A body without color. A body that wouldn't be despised. But in doing so, we created a body without compassion. The American Jesus has the ideal American body—healed, handsome, and hands off when it comes to the needs of the marginalized in Western society. When it comes to the American Jesus, the narrative has been changed from God creating us in his image to us creating him in our own.

By healing Jesus, we have raised an image—an idol, if you will. Like Micah, we have created an image of the god we would like to worship—a god that is more deserving of our undying devotion because a God who is disabled simply cannot be worshiped. Our ableist inclinations whisper to our souls that a God who is disabled cannot be trusted. We crave an image of God that projects our greatest desire, a world absent of disabled and despised bodies.

Bodies of Work

Exceptionalism, Ableism,
and Our Theology of Work

One day a young Levite, who had been living in Bethlehem in Judah, arrived in that area. He had left Bethlehem in search of another place to live, and as he traveled, he came to the hill country of Ephraim. He happened to stop at Micah's house as he was traveling through. "Where are you from?" Micah asked him. He replied, "I am a Levite from Bethlehem in Judah, and I am looking for a place to live." "Stay here with me," Micah said, "and you can be a father and priest to me. I will give you ten pieces of silver a year, plus a change of clothes and your food." The Levite agreed to this, and the young man became like one of Micah's sons.

—Judges 17:7–11

Like many people, I vividly remember the moments leading up to the global shutdown due to the coronavirus pandemic.

There had been minimal coverage about a deadly virus spreading across the globe. We didn't know much about the impact of what we would later come to know as COVID-19, especially its impact on the global economy.

News about a shutdown in Georgia came on a Friday evening. My wife, Isabella, who works for the Centers for Disease Control and Prevention, had already been deployed to New York to help screen international flights coming into the United States. I was attending the opening retreat for a three-year pastoral cohort I had recently joined. Our children were scheduled to spend the weekend with their respective friends while we were out of town. As far as we knew, everything would remain unchanged due to this virus.

Just a few hours after arriving at the retreat, several of my colleagues began fielding calls from church staff and members. Rumors were beginning to circulate about a possible shelter-in-place order. Up until that point, we heard news that just a few states had begun taking measures to try to circumvent the spread of this virus. To be frank, I was skeptical that a complete shutdown would be warranted, let alone implemented. Just as the sun began to set that Friday, the news flashed across my phone that the governor of Georgia had indeed issued a two-week shelter-in-place order that included asking all churches to limit in-person gatherings to ten people or less.

I don't pastor a megachurch, but we definitely had far more than ten people attending Sunday mornings. Needless to say, my pastoral colleagues and I scrambled to adjust. We didn't spend much time focusing on the retreat because the world as we knew it was about to change in ways we had yet to comprehend. There would be no church gathering that Sunday. There would be no choirs, no children's ministry, no greeting team, and no preaching. In forty-eight hours, our church buildings would be empty.

The global pandemic did a lot to expose the church to its ableist practices. When it became more apparent that large gatherings would be prohibited for far longer than two weeks, churches of all sizes mustered up the money and the creativity to implement strategies, technology, and even ecclesiology that helped them better meet the needs of those who suddenly couldn't access their facilities and programs. Streaming live services across social media platforms became standard practice, because accessibility rose to the top of churches' lists of ministry priorities.

Pastors, church leaders, and congregants all learned that the work of the church was going to have to change for it to survive a prolonged period of exclusively online worship. Since that time, many churches have returned to in-person worship while maintaining a thriving online ministry. Yet we must face the harsh reality that the accommodations and accessibility that some in the disability community now enjoy came only as a fortunate by-product of churches catering to the able-bodied when church buildings shut down.

Returning again to the story of Micah, we discover that much of what Micah does mirrors the way we have organized the church to prioritize able-bodiedness. The parallels between his story and ours don't just end at the doorstep of the church. These likenesses reverberate throughout society, mainly because of roots established early on in American Christianity. What Micah does is put our discrimination on full display.

In the above passage from Judges, Micah, who has already assigned his son as a priest, meets a Levite from Bethlehem. I can imagine Micah's delight as he meets a young man from the official priestly tribe of Levi. Micah wastes no time, and we can see a few things that serve to highlight the impact of ableism and religion on the concept of work.

First, Micah invites the young priest to take up residence in his home. Keep in mind that Micah has already established the images and idols that inform his religious devotion. Next, he offers the Levite a salary and initially defines their relationship as one in which the Levite will exercise influence and authority on himself, by asking him to "be a father and priest" (v. 10) to him. The next verse is interesting because although the Levite agrees, he eventually becomes "like one of Micah's sons" (v. 11). Finally, Micah assumes that the blessing of God rests on his version of religious devotion.

Ableism works the same process. The priest is hired to serve the images and idols that Micah has already established. Ableism establishes images and idols of acceptable humans, humans that are often able-bodied, and insists that both religion and employment surrender to the ultimate rule of those images. As we learned during the pandemic, many churches provided accessibility through online worship and other creative means—not because they wanted to include the disability community but rather to serve the established images and idols of able-bodied Christians who couldn't otherwise access their services.

The relationship between Micah and the Levite also illustrates a very subtle aspect of ableism and its impact on employment. Micah, although needing (and requesting) spiritual parentage from the priest, as was their custom, ended up treating the priest like his child. Ableism is drenched in paternalism. Disabled people, even when given opportunities, are still often infantilized, becoming like sons and daughters of their more capable and more intelligent counterparts both in the church and in the workforce.

This isn't just an issue within Christian faith, although Christianity has certainly influenced it. We can see the relationship between disability and employment play out in the larger society, especially in the moments following the slow dissipation of the pandemic. One of the most obvious ways we experienced this is with the rise in telecommuting or work-from-home opportunities due to the need to socially distance.

When new safety protocols were put into place, many workplaces began asking their employees to work from home. Remote working actually contributed to a significant shift in employment culture in the United States. According to research done by the Economic Innovation Group, individuals with disabilities between the ages of twenty-five and fifty-four were 3.5 percent more likely to hold employment in the second quarter of 2022 than before the pandemic. While the study admits there are other factors to consider, such as a national labor shortage, the fact remains that the rise in openness to remote work after the pandemic has made a significant dent in the high unemployment rates among disabled Americans. Gus Alexiou, a contributor to Forbes, writes, "In many ways, Covid-19 super-charged and mainstreamed a shift of corporate mindsets in relation to remote work, and individuals with disabilities have been among the prime beneficiaries."[1] While this may be true, the cultural shift to remote work was not the result of decades of lobbying by the disability community to have equal and equitable access to the workforce. Similar to the churches that made accessibility a priority during the pandemic, many workplaces seemingly stumbled into providing accommodations that disabled people are just happening to benefit from.

When the image of what a productive worker resembled changed, the vehicle of production adapted, but ableism was at the root of the entire shift because persons with disabilities are always dependent on the integrity and influence of the idol makers who lead these institutions. Our ideology about work has one agenda: living in service to the images of the preferred human body and mind.

Ableism and the Appearance of Productivity

Over the last two decades, I have become intimately familiar with ableism, especially as it relates to employment. As a Black autistic man, traversing this path is often doubly difficult because of the continued link between disability and Blackness. Being autistic presents a number of challenges in gaining and maintaining meaningful employment. Images and idols of what it means to be normal and employable stand watch at the employment gate. The barriers begin during the interview process. The typical process for gaining employment (unless you are given a position, like Micah gave one to his son) is a serious discussion with strangers about your qualifications and prior experience. For me, going to unknown spaces and meeting unfamiliar people can be a gigantic barrier due to social anxiety. An interview typically lasts somewhere between thirty minutes and one hour, during this time the applicant shoulders the burden of convincing the gatekeeper that they are likeable. In what should be an impartial search for qualified applicants who possess the skills and experience to hold the position, the interview actually becomes a system by which employers look to hire those who most closely fit their own image and who are most likely to serve and support the broader system that produces subsequent image bearers. Simply put, employers claim to be searching for labor and loyalty, but the entry process doesn't always let autistic people demonstrate their capabilities.

Before I continue, I will pause here to acknowledge the privilege I have that many disabled people do not have. As someone who currently holds a high-level position, my story is not the norm. That said, it took me nearly two decades to ascend to a place of leadership in my chosen profession; ableism, especially within the ranks of clergy, has created consistent barriers to my accomplishments.

At no point, however, have I become more keenly aware of my own challenges with ableism than when I began to experience an increase in physical limitations due to both my cancer and my cancer treatments. Chemotherapy did a number on my body, leaving me with severe neuropathy in my feet. Over the past few years, the pain has become more pronounced, leaving me constantly between an eight and a ten on a pain scale of ten being the worst. Needless to say, this has slowed me down quite a bit. I am not nearly as mobile as I was, and after two years of experimenting with different medications and therapy regimens, it appears as though the nerve damage will be permanent. Other forms of treatment, including surgery, have also caused me to begin living with new physical limitations. As I write this chapter, I am still very much in the heat of my second battle with colorectal cancer, and it has taken a toll on my body.

The last few years have probably, at least pastorally, been what I consider to be the least productive years of my life. I have not been able to accomplish as much as I would have liked. I have had to limit the number of activities that I engage in. I'm not nearly as present at my church as I would like to be, and many of the goals that I set for my church and my professional life have yet to be accomplished. I have realized that when you are persuaded that productivity equals value, it becomes difficult to be satisfied with your life.

But the truth is that fatigue, pain, lack of mobility, and a host of other challenges related to cancer have at times slowed me to a complete halt. There are many days when my body just is not capable of completing more than one meaningful task. I don't have the same energy or focus that I once had, and all of this is in addition to the sensory-processing issues and social anxiety that are often associated with my autism.

I realized how much my life had been shaped by internalized ableism when I found myself struggling with not being able to live up to the images and idols that American Christianity has created for pastoral leaders. I had already struggled with the social aspects of pastoring, but after my autism diagnosis in 2014, I became more open about my experiences and drew appropriate boundaries for myself and the congregations I served. I had slowly worked my way into neither living up to or downwind of people's unrealistic expectations of me. When cancer came, I experienced something different.

Ableism will coax you into believing that your greatest potential is found only in serving the image. This becomes doubly true when you attach your spirituality to ableism's image. In America, we like to believe that our biases are long behind us when it comes to who can serve as God's prophets and preachers, but just look at who gets to sell the most books, pastor the largest churches, speak at the most popular conferences, and enjoy the most trust in Christianity. Ableism keeps a tight rein on the products and producers of Christian content. This is why it is so infuriating that like many people, I fell for it. Although I had been open about being autistic, my own sense of resistance to living up to and in service of these images was compromised, and it took battling cancer for me to realize it.

In chapter 1 above, when talking about the dawn of definitions of disability in America, I discussed how the Puritan social order was shaped by two primary social, religious, and economic ideals: family and farming. This order provided the Puritans with the necessary structure to organize their culture and their Christian practice by ranking which bodies best served the needs of their economic pursuits. I would argue that the influence that their religious perspective placed on the ranking of bodies is still prevalent today.

What springs from the depths of defining and ranking bodies according to their ability to produce is a sense of exceptionalism that permeates our cultural norms and traditions. Bodies that can benefit from capitalism are in fact the very types of bodies that have access to the pathway of exceptionalism. Productive bodies and minds are simultaneously celebrated and exploited for their labor and intellectual property. When bodies are unable to produce in ways that bolster the economy, they are considered dispensable. They are viewed as liabilities. They are labeled disabled. Living with cancer and its limitations exposed me to just how much ableism thrives on a generalized lack of creativity in discerning the contributions of bodies that have been labeled as liabilities to the institution called work.

Although the growing acceptance of remote work has made employment slightly more accessible for the disability community, we still must strongly consider how remote work only opened the door more widely to the already existing job categories that the institution has produced. Those jobs are still influenced by the same Puritan ethic that has shaped the definition of disability and the declaration of the bodies that are most beneficial to its goals. In other words, the entire institution of employment was never designed to take the time to discover and deploy the talents, skills, and experiences of disabled bodies. The jobs that exist as part of our capitalist system are the result of the influence of ableist ideology.

Perhaps this is the reason that I became overwhelmed with guilt and insecurity when I was not able to efficiently and consistently fulfill my duties as a pastor at my church while battling cancer twice in a three-year span. The role of clergy has never been exempted from the influence of ableism. There is a definite image that serves the institution of the church, and there are definitely prescribed pastoral characteristics and traits that shape the likelihood that a person can succeed in that role. One of the primary expressions of this ableist influence is what is so often referred to as "grind culture."

The Gospel of Grind Culture

One of the most subtle and damaging evangelical teachings that arose from early Puritan theology is the idea that our bodies are inherently bad. The New Testament describes a battle between the Spirit and the flesh, and it's a prominent theme in the Pastoral Epistles, attributed to the apostle Paul. For years, I used to believe that the primary interpretation of those texts and this concept was that the flesh, or our bodies, would lead us astray unless we kept them firmly in check. The role of faith, as Paul says in 1 Corinthians 9:27, was to "beat my body into submission." The Spirit's job was to take control of my body and to redirect it into doing its bidding, oftentimes a bidding that was supposed to demonstrate the depths of my belief in God and my commitment to living a life of faith and service to him.

The contest between the Spirit and the flesh can be difficult to digest when you live with a disability. We hear the message that our bodies are ultimately accountable to our spirits. The inability to control our bodies is often seen as a failure of faith. Now, I know that many people will suggest that the point of such passages from Paul (or whoever wrote the text) is that the contest between flesh and spirit is primarily about the need to subdue our desires, most often the sinful desires that we have. The idea that nothing good dwells in our flesh isn't so much about our physical bodies and the capabilities of those bodies as it is about the Spirit's authority over sinful desires. More often than not, these ideas have been used to communicate a need for a Christian sexual ethic.

While there may be some truth in needing our faith to assist us with curbing unhealthy sexual desires, I still contend that the overall message that the body is inherently bad or evil is one that has different implications for those living with disabilities or chronic illnesses. Disability and cancer don't always allow me to exercise power over my body, and if sexual ethics is the only use for those passages of Scripture, then we very well may be ignoring the fact that sexual desires are not the only messages that our bodies send to us. In all honesty, I believe that we know this to be a reality, although we seldom address this tainted teaching for what it is—ableist. When our bodies are communicating pain, fatigue, or other serious issues to us, the denial of the flesh is not a virtue; it is actually dangerous.

Being limited by cancer caused me to interrogate my battle with my body when it was clearly communicating to me that working in the same way that I was previously able to operate was no longer an option. So where did my guilt and shame come from? Ableism. I learned to patiently listen to and participate with what my body required of me in the moment and in each day and season of my life. Denying the signals that my body is sending me—for my own good—I have learned, is an act of violence against the image of God in me. We need our bodies, and we don't need to compete with them.

This is why grind culture is so incessantly evil and ableist at its core. Grind culture, also known as hustle culture, is the idea that achievement and success are based on high levels of productivity. Grind culture not only encourages working long hours and ignoring the needs of the body for rest; it actually uses the lack of rest as a metric for success. Overworking and overextending oneself in the pursuit of personal and professional goals is a badge of honor in grind culture. The body is a tool to be dominated in order to achieve maximum production and maximum profit. The engine that drives grind culture is its promise of reaching the apex of one's industry. It is the bootstrap mentality on performance-enhancing drugs. If you want to be considered a success, you have to demonstrate your willingness to deny your body or, in the language of Christianity, deny your flesh.

In my opinion, Christian principles have been inappropriately hijacked in support of this toxic trend. For Christians, denying the flesh in service of a greater good at work is seen as a spiritual badge of honor, the value of which exceeds any monetary gain. For many Christians, the ultimate public act of faith is to work tirelessly for the cause, giving one's body over to a proverbial crucifixion week in and week out in an effort to prove how close one is to God. In this way of practicing faith, the body becomes more of a barrier to ultimate spiritual fulfillment than anything else.

But work without rest isn't God's design for the human body. In fact, the sum total of our spiritual experience is filtered through the bodies that God has given us and the limits those bodies possess. The Sabbath is God's guard against grind culture. After the Israelites had spent countless years laboring for Pharaoh, being made to produce more with fewer resources, it's no wonder God instituted the Sabbath for them. Grind culture is ableist because it automatically excludes those who don't have the luxury of denying their body the right to be obeyed.

One of the unexpected gifts of having to slow down during cancer treatments was the realization that ministry work, or work in general, need not be influenced by an unhealthy relationship to our God-given bodies. There is a great spiritual truth that those who live with disabilities can teach the church. Production does not equal worth. When I was unable to work, to produce, to be an asset to my church, and to drive profits, our entire community learned the sacredness of allowing God to define work not as a function of profit-making but as a vehicle for place-making (belonging for all based on God's creative and cooperative design). Ironically, when my production was at its lowest was when I felt most at home with my congregation. As a disabled pastor, I have been challenged by an internalized ableism that drove me to constantly seek to contribute enough to my church and to Christianity so as to justify my calling and career. It was in the trenches of a life-altering battle with cancer that I experienced the grace that is abundant when place-making as a work of the church becomes more of a goal than profit- and production-making. During this low point, I found a true place in the church and a true home in the shadows of God's holy design for humanity.

Developing a healthy, nonableist theology of work begins with understanding the role of work. In the story of creation, God's work is the work of place-making. God, in his infinite wisdom, recognizes the chaos that compromises his creation, and in recognizing the looming threat of this chaos, God begins his eternal work by pushing back the chaos, pushing back the darkness that distorts our sense of purpose and sense of place. This is the essence of God's work in the world. The story of God's creation isn't merely about sin. It begins with a God who works tirelessly to create a place for creation to reflect his glorious image.

In the beginning, God's declaration of place-making, his sacred work, is initiated with the words "Let there be." The language of being is central to understanding a more spiritually enriching theology of work, one that does not simply view bodies as products to be consumed but as cocreators of sacred space. "Let there be" is a declaration about existence and about the importance of the forthcoming human experience. God values being over doing.

In the creation narrative, when God creates human beings, he does so by pushing back the darkness and by making space for his creation to be a part of the process. Rachel Marie Kang, author of *Let There Be Art: The Pleasure and Purpose of Unleashing the Creativity within You*, writes, "God, in his infinite power, plans a partnership with man in this work of pushing back the darkness, long before he even breathes life into man's lungs."[2] Hebrew Bible scholar Jeffery M. Leonard states that "God charges humankind with taking up the divine mantle of creating and working to push back the boundaries of this chaos still further."[3] Ableism robs humanity of the creativity needed to include all types of bodies in the divine work of rolling back the darkness and chaos that threatens the splendor of God's light. In fact, ableism could be considered one of the primary contributors to the darkness and chaos that God is inviting his creation to resist because it assumes that the work of pushing back the darkness doesn't require disabled bodies. It places

the burden of the work on the shoulders of a few bodies
that are exceptional. Nearly every faith community experiences this reality as the eighty-twenty rule. Eighty percent
of the work is done by 20 percent of the people. But what
if that statistic is a symptom of ableism? What if it is the
result of creating categories within our faith communities
that exclude certain bodies?

In a previous chapter about the Black church, we introduced the idea that not only does ableism exclude certain
bodies; it also tends to exclude certain bodies of work that
derive from those bodies and minds. The work of pushing
back the chaos and the darkness requires a variety of ideas
and perspectives. In the process of creating a system to roll
back the chaos, God creates a wide variety of species, even
prior to creating humanity in his image. The God of creation is the God of variety. Each uniquely designed creation
serves a critical purpose in the work of place-making. This
means that at no point can we seriously consider a concept
of work that does not take into consideration the value of
the various ways that different bodies experience the call
to curb the chaos.

Capitalism assumes that some will be excluded from the
institution of employment. By contrast, a theology of work
centered on place-making rather than profit-making will
include a variety of bodies, in the same way that the creation
narrative centers variety as a primary feature in separating the dark from the light and the purpose of life from the
chaos of death. With a theology of place-making, disability
is seen not as a liability for the workforce but rather as a
necessity. The success of the institution of work is dependent on disabled and other minority bodies, because with

those bodies come the bodies of work that infuse the world with ideas, strategies, and creativity that make work more than a system of production and more of a call to make place for God's creation.

American Christianity needs an infusion of place-making over and against profit-making. Disability theology, the theological body of work being produced by disabled scholars and theologians, is often seen as merely a celebration of difference. Disability theology is more than that: it's an exploration of God's embodied human experience and the way that the incarnation of deity both interrogates and informs humanity's experience with God. The ideas that spring forth from this body of work are necessary for Christianity and for the future of race relations in our society.

The incarnation is a part of God's extraordinary effort to continually push back the darkness and chaos that threaten human relationships. In the ultimate act of securing a place for humanity, God inhabits a limited human body, demonstrating his connection to and appreciation for the human body. In order to make the shift from an ableist and purely capitalistic view of work, more Christians should welcome the variety of bodies and bodies of work that God has commissioned to curb the chaos. Those bodies are bodies that are different, bodies that are disabled, and bodies that have been considered disabled because of their skin color. Christian theology and churches should include and study disability theology, not just seeking answers to why certain bodies "don't work" or to assess which bodies aren't "well" or which bodies belong at the bottom of the body hierarchy, but rather to explore how God works through a variety of bodies and the different types of work they produce. In this way, we afford ourselves the best possible opportunity to learn more about God's divinity and God's desire to include humanity in his work of pushing back the darkness of able-ism and racism.

Disability, the Cross, and Unraveling Shame

Remembering Jesus and Reimagining Disability

The Body-Image Battle

I have shared earlier in these pages that in the fall of 2020, I was diagnosed with stage 3 cancer. After only a year of remission, the cancer came back. Getting the news that my cancer had returned was disappointing, for sure, but the recurrence rate for the type of cancer I have is 50 percent. I just happened to be on the wrong side of the statistic.

My ongoing battle with cancer has been emotionally, mentally, and spiritually challenging. If you're reading this and have experienced this journey, then you are keenly aware that this battle can slowly erode your mental and spiritual reserves. Every day brings about decisions that deplete both your focus and your faith. When you're facing the beast called cancer, there is no faith to borrow for tomorrow's trials. The path in front of you, in the present, takes every ounce of faith you can possibly muster, and it leaves nothing for the next day. Battling cancer is truly a daily walk of faith.

Then there are the physical limitations. At the time of my first diagnosis, I was told by one of my doctors that because I was young and relatively healthy, they were going to "throw the kitchen sink at me." This meant they were going to use every medical tool at their disposal to cure me of my cancer. Radiation and chemotherapy are both the perfect paradox. The technology and medicine that can save lives can also drastically alter them. Like many people who have been in my position, I have a complicated relationship with the tools used to treat cancer. Don't get me wrong: I am grateful to be here. I am blessed to still be breathing, especially when so many others who have walked this weary path have not experienced the success that I have. At the same time, the treatment has made life difficult.

Chemotherapy does significant damage to your nerve endings. During treatment, doctors tell you that you will be extremely sensitive to the cold. That is an understatement if there ever was one. The tips of my fingers and toes often felt like they were being dipped in liquid nitrogen at the slightest breeze that would enter the room. By the time I would rise from my chair in the infusion center after hours of chemo pumping through my body, even the movement of my limbs was enough to create pain in my hands and feet because simply walking down the hall created a cool sensation that pressed against my fragile skin.

Several months of chemotherapy caused significant damage to my feet. Most days, the pain is a nine on a scale of ten. The pain is an odd combination of feelings, including the type of numbness and tingling that you experience when your circulation is cut off. You know, the pins and needles feeling. It also feels like an intense burning, the likes of which most have never felt. This significant pain doesn't just have an impact on my feet; it also impacts the way that my joints work because the pain has changed the way I walk. I constantly have problems with my ankles, knees, and hips, and this has also made it challenging to exercise.

During my nearly yearlong treatment for cancer the first time (at the time of writing, I am awaiting the start of my second battle with cancer), I gained over thirty pounds. In addition to not exercising, I fell into bad eating habits, primarily because I only ate what I could actually taste, which was often unhealthy foods. I also had to take steroids to help with my immune system, because the treatments left my body vulnerable. All of this was taking place during the height of a global pandemic, which made dealing with the changes in my body difficult, to say the least.

In June 2021, I underwent surgery to remove what remained of the cancerous tumor following treatment. Surgery required several hours of complex reorganizing of my body. I'll spare you the details, but just know that removing cancer and resecting the colon and rectum changes the way the body works. Dramatically. Even a year after the surgery, my body is still adjusting to the new way it has to operate in the absence of what was once there. In addition to all of the inward changes, the surgery (done robotically) left me with five small horizontal scars across my abdomen. I also had to have a procedure to place the port catheter in my chest so that I can receive chemotherapy intravenously. The scars from that surgery are also visible. Then, in the spring of 2023, I was rushed to the hospital with severe abdominal pain and was admitted to the hospital for a large bowel obstruction. The next morning, I had a lifesaving emergency surgery that left me with a six-inch vertical scar on my abdomen and a permanent colostomy.

Why am I sharing all of this? Because for years I have struggled with body image. Even when I was at the height of my physical fitness as a college football player, I was rarely satisfied with the way my body looked. Over the years, I've struggled with my appearance. I suppose a large part of my self-consciousness is due to social anxiety. I don't like being the center of attention. I loathe being stared at and struggle with thoughts of how I am being perceived. Autism has obviously had a role in these feelings, but what I discovered about myself is that shame has a particular stronghold on my life when it relates to how others view my body. I discovered this when I found myself frantically trying to hide the scars and the other changes in my body that cancer has caused.

I could say more about the emotional and spiritual toll that cancer takes, but for this chapter, I want to engage the very real changes that battling cancer has brought upon my body and the very real ways that physical ailments, chronic illness, and disability challenge perceptions of the human body. This chapter is about taking on the challenge of societal shame by taking a deeper look at the role, response, and residue of the crucifixion of Jesus.

Voices of Resistance

In the story of Micah and his mother (Judg. 17), Micah returns the stolen money to his mother in order to avoid a curse. If there is anything that is commonly true about human nature, it is that when possible, we always choose to avoid embarrassment. Shame is a powerful force that has severe consequences. Micah returns the stolen money because he wants to avoid the shame and embarrassment of living under a curse. Nothing in the story in Judges convinces me that Micah returns what he has stolen as a result of a genuine conviction about his sin. Nothing in his actions demonstrates that he returns the stolen money as an act of repentance. He is motivated by shame, and in the end, shame is a poor substitute for both personal repentance and systemic change.

The story of ableism in American history is one that lacks the important work of shedding the shame and stigma associated with the marginalization of Black and disabled bodies. Using disability as the primary vehicle for perpetuating racial slavery created a residue that has extended the toxicity of body shame beyond direct racial bias. In the beginning, the prioritizing of bodies, mainly White male bodies deemed nondisabled, by default created an entire category of "other" that was not only to be avoided but to be shamed. Being on the outside of what was considered both socially and spiritually normal created a shroud of shame. Stolen African bodies carried the burden of the shame and stain of racial slavery.

Black theology, born out of the historically Black church, sheds light on the stigma and shame associated with racial slavery by having a unique perspective about God, the incarnation, and the cross. In the early days of the Black church, preachers would help their congregants find a sense of dignity by helping them to imagine God not as a White man, as was so often presented to them by their oppressors, but as a Black man, who could intimately identify with their experience of marginalization.

Black liberation theology has not gone without its fair share of critics. Many consider liberation theology to be controversial and too liberal. I've often heard critiques of Black liberation theology that quite honestly sound eerily similar to recent critiques of critical race theory (CRT). Of the many critiques that both liberation theology and CRT receive, the most prevalent, usually from the White evangelical church, is that they are incompatible with the gospel.

Before we move on, I should note that CRT is not the primary subject of this chapter. In fact, CRT is, in my opinion, not a primary topic discussed in many historically Black churches today. Many of my Black clergy colleagues never even engaged with CRT until it became an issue among White evangelical churches and pastors. CRT is not a theology. It is a theory. It is a theory that arose within graduate-level legal courses in an attempt to explain the inefficiency that laws have historically played in ridding American culture of structural and systemic racism. With that being said, there should be a strong consideration of the consistent response to any theology or theory that pushes back against a long-standing history of Eurocentric, able-bodied, male-dominated perspectives about God, Scripture, and the application of the teachings of Jesus. Both

Black liberation theology and disability theology share this in common, and they are often rejected and labeled with the most up-to-date terminology aimed at framing these ideas as a false or substandard version of Christianity.

Here's the problem: nearly all of the early theological positions posited by European colonists in American Christian history have proven to be invalid and, more strongly put, unbiblical. According to scholar and historian Jemar Tisby, many Christian denominations in early America made conscious decisions to develop doctrine that supported racial slavery. In *The Color of Compromise* he writes, "The Virginia Assembly took the initiative to enact a new law. Despite the established tradition, the assembly decided that baptism would not confer freedom upon their laborers. Instead, Africans would remain in physical bondage even after their conversion." Adjusting the Bible and doctrine to support discrimination was a common occurrence among Christian churches in the colonial period. Tisby goes on, "From the beginning of American colonization, Europeans crafted a Christianity that would allow them to spread the faith without confronting the exploitative economic system of slavery and the emerging social inequality based on color."[1] It's also true that theological positions were taken that Black bodies and disabled bodies were inherently inferior to White bodies and minds that were defined as able-bodied. Ableism and racism in early American history functioned because of ideas introduced by Christians. Readings and applications of the biblical text were designed to subjugate an entire population of people. Theology was twisted to support ableism, racism, sexism, and capitalism, and it was used to benefit a protected class of people.

The question should be asked: With all of the evidence we have of the inaccuracies of early Eurocentric Christian theology, why do we continue to reject the theological perspectives of minorities in America? I believe the answer is that American Christianity still has an avoidance issue. American Christianity works extremely hard to avoid the reality that it has accomplished exactly what it set out to accomplish—the creation of a religious and racial hierarchy that has placed Black and disabled bodies at the bottom of the social order. American Christianity isn't broken because it is working the way it was designed to work. Avoidance is a mechanism used to reject the lived experience, and the theology born out of that lived experience is aimed at toppling Western Christianity in the same way that the incarnate God, Jesus, toppled the Roman Empire.

Avoidance is a form of rejection that uses shame to control and to quench the holy prophetic fire that is being fanned into flame by the bodies and minds of those who have been marginalized and punished for not being White or able-bodied. To avoid those bodies and minds is to place them in theological exile, banishing them to ministry on the margins and forcing them to live in a theologically liminal space meant to limit their prophetic value—Black and disabled people who are committed followers of Jesus and who, in many ways, are more accurate practitioners of his teachings.

The issue we must deal with is the systemic use of shame as a tool to control those voices or, at the very least, to control how the majority of evangelical Christian culture views and values those voices on the margins. In *Reading While Black: African American Biblical Interpretation as an Exercise in Hope,* Esau McCaulley suggests that African American interpretation of the biblical text has always been one that is deeply rooted in African Americans' social location, a location that they believed brought them to a profound understanding of Scripture and the God of Scripture and that served as their defense against the shame that slavery sought to bestow upon them because of their skin color and social location. He writes, "The social location of enslaved persons caused them to read the Bible differently. This unabashedly *located* reading had marked African American interpretation since."[2]

In many ways, Black and disabled readings of the biblical text are the genesis of rebelling against the shame and stigma that American Christianity has placed on minority bodies. Enslaved Africans rebelled against the use of Scripture to subjugate them to their White enslavers by developing their own robust and rebellious readings of the Bible that cultivated a sense of resistance to shame, which is necessary in all religious reformation. Black and disabled bodies are not obligated to accept interpretations of sacred texts that further disenfranchise them, and to assume that they should merely accept those interpretations and applications is, in fact, a large part of the arrogance of ableism, racism, and sexism.

Central to the reinterpretation of texts that shatter the historical use of shame against Black and disabled bodies is a radical reinterpretation of the relationship of the cross and the power of control and shame. Christ followers who have been shoved to the margins have long seen the cross as a central point of God's intentional identification with systemic attempts to place shame on the bodies of those who fail to live up to the standards of normalcy. But since the inception of Christianity, marginalized followers of Jesus have continually developed the creativity and imagination needed to transform tools of oppression and symbols of shame into symbols of resistance. McCaulley writes, "In the strange economy of the kingdom, the cross is glory. But who then is the first bearer of the cross other than our Lord?"[3]

Roman crucifixion was a fairly common tool used to maintain control of all the subjects of the Roman Empire, so while Christianity claims a close connection to crucifixion, Christians are the only religious group that maintains a complicated relationship with crucifixion. What is important to note in the context of Christian conversations about the cross is the connection that exists because of the Gospel narratives about Jesus, the central figure of the Christian faith, and his death by Roman torture and crucifixion. For most Christians, the story of crucifixion is important because it is the story of one man who is crucified. That man was Jesus, and because of the Gospel narratives and their claims about the true identity of Jesus, Christians tend to place all of their attention on him. No doubt the story of Roman crucifixion is a fascinating one, but Christians are singularly focused on Jesus and his experience. McCaulley contends that based on a long-standing tradition of African American biblical interpretation, Black people in America have also made a profound connection to the story of Jesus being crucified because of the presence of an African man named Simon. According to the Gospel of Mark, Simon was from Cyrene, a city in North Africa in what is now modern-day Libya. It is without question that Simon was a dark-skinned African man who, Mark writes, was "forced . . . to carry Jesus' cross" (Mark 15:21).

Carrying crosses isn't a new experience for Black and disabled bodies. Crosses have been forced upon them for centuries. Our culture and our churches continue to burden them with crosses of shame and stigma. Evangelical Christians have an ever-present need to avoid the consequences of being complicit in helping to establish a system that perpetuates bias against bodies that are considered abnormal. This is why, for many minority bodies (including bodies deemed disabled by ableist ideology), crucifixion has long been a symbol of the systems that society has used to shame and, in many cases, disable and disenfranchise.

When it comes to understanding how the religious experiences of Black people in America have influenced a theology anchored in the liberation motifs found in the Bible, there is perhaps no greater resource than the late doctor James H. Cone (1938–2018). Cone is often credited with the expansion of liberation theology into mainstream seminaries and universities by introducing many to a Black theology of liberation. He is often regarded as one of America's most esteemed theologians, and he published a number of books that examine Christian themes through the lens of Black life in America. One of his most prominent books, *The Cross and the Lynching Tree*, explores the radical relationship that African Americans once had with one of the most terrifying tools of slavery and Jim Crow in America—lynching.

According to Cone, Black religious life in America was dominated by its connection between the cross of Christ and the lynching tree of America. For Cone, Black life, both inside and outside the church, was deeply shaped by the ability of Black folks to see Jesus as the God who is intimately acquainted with the horrors of the lynching tree and who also demonstrates love for humanity and the suffering of those who have been marginalized. In Black theology, God is not only on the side of the oppressed, but God also decides, in Jesus, to become one of them, making the cross an instrument by which all suffering and shame is absorbed by the Suffering Servant, as portrayed in Mark's Gospel.

Cone was convinced that the important connection between the cross and the lynching tree should be evident, yet American Christianity lacked the theological imagination to see it. He writes, "The crucifixion of Jesus by the Romans in Jerusalem and the lynching of blacks by whites in the United States are so amazingly similar that one wonders what blocks the American Christian imagination from seeing the connection."[4] In a similar way, the connection between disability and human limitation and the postresurrection body of Jesus are so strikingly similar that we should also ask, What blocks American Christianity from exercising the type of imagination that aids in seeing the connection? The answer to both questions is shame. Like Micah, America has avoided connecting symbols of racism and ableism to God because it continues to displace the shame of its initial sin onto the bodies of those it sinned against.

Disregarding Shame

Therefore, since we are surrounded by such a huge crowd of witnesses to the life of faith, let us strip off every weight that slows us down, especially the sin that so easily trips us up. And let us run with endurance the race God has set before us. We do this by keeping our eyes on Jesus, the champion who initiates and perfects our faith. *Because of the joy awaiting him*, he endured the cross, *disregarding its shame*. Now he is seated in the place of honor beside God's throne.

—Hebrews 12:1–2 (emphasis added)

Black liberation theology has infused American Christianity with the much-needed and sorely lacking imagination that is necessary for correcting its initial sin of racial slavery. At the same time, embracing disability theology is a necessary tool for engaging the images and institutions that early American Christianity produced. Disability has long been seen as a celebration of different bodies—a vehicle for providing disabled people with dignity and honor within the Christian tradition and the broader society. Except disabled people are already worthy of dignity and honor. Disability theology is not just a celebration of difference; it is also an exploration of God's embodied human experience while simultaneously interrogating and informing humanity's experience with God.

The doctrine of incarnation is the story of a God who is born, a God who bleeds, and a God who is buried in a human body. God's connection with and appreciation for the human body is perhaps the most important element of our faith. Disability theology is not just a novelty. It is essential to Christianity, particularly in the Western world. Able-bodied Christians should study disability theology not just to answer questions related to why certain bodies don't work or why certain bodies aren't well; instead, disability theology serves as a means of exploring how God works through bodies—*all* bodies. Christians can actually learn more about the divinity of Jesus that way. As we close this chapter, I want to highlight the value of disability theology and its connection to dismantling systemic shame and stigma against Black and disabled bodies.

Cone's work in *The Cross and the Lynching Tree* lights the way forward in combining disability theology and Black theology as they intersect at the site of Jesus's crucifixion. According to the writer of Hebrews, Jesus knew full well the shame and stigma associated with crucifixion. In fact, anyone living during his time would understand that the brutality of the cross was designed to dehumanize its victims. The horrors of crucifixion were utilized to shame and to control the population. This was particularly true for the Jewish people living under Roman oppression because of their long-held belief that dying on a tree was a curse (Deut. 21:22–23).

For as much as death on a cross itself was considered a curse, the road to the cross was much more embarrassing for Jesus than the typical execution of criminals in the Roman Empire. Jesus was denied the dignity of a just trial. Like many Black and disabled people, Jesus can identify with a political system that failed to afford him the right to be treated fairly and equally in the eyes of the law. Jesus went through a mockery of a trial and was given a death sentence. He was also brutally beaten, which means that his state-sponsored, disabling torture was a lesson, a message of sorts to the masses that the empire uses maiming and disabling as a means to place shame on the bodies of its marginalized. Disabling the body of Jesus—in other words, disabling God—was the plan of the empire, and it has influenced the role of religion and politics in modern expressions of Christianity.

Unlike Micah, however, Jesus isn't placed under a curse for his own sin, and unlike Micah, Jesus doesn't seek to avoid the issue of initial sin. Jesus takes on the sin of the world, and most importantly, he doesn't defer to shame. Rather, he *disregards* the shame of the cross. God incarnate—God embodied—models for us how to destroy the disabling effects of the curse of shame, which has been forced upon Black and disabled bodies. It was the joy awaiting Jesus, the writer of Hebrews says, that motivated him to endure the cross and to disregard the shame associated with death on a tree.

Joy is an underrated and underutilized tool in Christian formation. Oftentimes, we think of joy as the product of something enjoyable; however, Jesus, in his purpose of addressing the initial sin of humanity, endured the cross because of joy. Willie James Jennings has defined *joy* as the work of resistance to the forces of despair and death.[5] Much of this book has been aimed at examining the history and theology that shaped the intersection between Black and disabled bodies and the way that the Christian church in the West has failed in its treatment of atypical bodies. In the conclusion, we'll take a look at Jesus, joy, and justice as a meaningful response to all we've discussed.

CONCLUSION

Jesus, Joy, and Justice

Discussing Initial Sin

In the summer of 2022, I discovered that the stage 3 colorectal cancer that was once in remission had returned. The news was disappointing, to say the least. I vividly recall how numb my body went as the doctor gave my wife and me the news that I would once again have to fight for my life. I felt as though my body was betraying me. It seemed as though the last year of my life was repeating itself. All of the treatments and all of the trauma were recycling themselves, setting a new course for my body that disregarded my self-determination to live well.

In the fall of 2020, when I was diagnosed with cancer for the first time, I had to subject my body to a vast number of medications and medical procedures. Between vaccines for my immune-compromised body, the placement of a port catheter in my chest, powerful radiation, and dozens of rounds of chemotherapy in pill form and through infusion, I was honestly starting to become disappointed that I hadn't developed any superpowers. I mean, isn't that the origin story for most comic book heroes? A medical procedure gone wrong. A powerful dose of radiation. An illness that turns into a genetic mutation. I would have thought I'd become a supersoldier or at the very least a hulk! Unfortunately, I cannot undo what cancer and life have done to my body. With the exception of things directly related to diet and exercise, the body that I inhabit now is unlikely to ascend to abilities beyond what is normal for me. People living with disabilities need the space and the support to be able to confidently make the same declaration. We are neither superhuman nor a subset of humanity. We are human.

Discussions about abilities and disabilities are often difficult terrain to navigate. There are no universal answers, principles, or steps to take in order to address ableism and the racism it supports because disability itself is reflective of such a wide range of experiences. Every person who has a disability experiences the world differently. In fact, in the field of disability studies, contributors often lament about the way disabilities are placed under one umbrella, which can have the negative consequence of erasing the uniqueness of each person's experience. Yet if you're like me and most Christians in the Western world, you want to know what to do about everything you've read in this book. What steps should we take? How can we develop a more disability-inclusive faith community? How can we practice antiableism and antiracism in our personal and congregational lives? These are all important and necessary questions to ask. Topics like ableism and racism and learning the history behind how we view the world can be overwhelming. For that reason, I want to begin the conclusion of this book by first pointing to the power and promise of joy as a tool in the work of being authentically antiableist.

In the beginning of this book, I shared with you what I called the "big three" of bias—initial sin, images and idols, and institutions. We've used these ideas to draw parallels between the story of Micah and the story of ableism in American Christianity. Hopefully, you have noticed that I have taken careful consideration in my assessment of the role of sin in relation to disability. In fact, I have chosen to categorize the first of the three biases as initial sin, not because it helps with the alliteration (although it does work out quite nicely); instead, I have chosen to label it as such as a way of challenging some of the ideas that are associated with the doctrine of original sin.

In case you're not familiar with the concept of original sin, let me explain that it is rooted in the idea that when Adam and Eve disobeyed God's instructions not to eat any fruit from the Tree of the Knowledge of Good and Evil, it released sin into the world, thus making every human subject to the consequences of sin. The story of creation is the story of the intersection and interaction between God and creation. When we read the creation narrative, we are observing the way a specific culture understood their relationship with God and goodness in the world. We don't have to be the writers of this ancient text to identify with it because, as humans, we all create narratives about our understanding of God and of goodness. We want to believe that we can understand the origin and nature of goodness.

But the truth is we can't. If the story of Eden teaches us anything, it's that we can't possess the knowledge of good and evil, and more importantly, we aren't designed to be able to handle it.

This is what makes the doctrine of original sin so troubling when it comes to understanding disability. Assuming that disability is a direct result of the fall of humankind is an easy and, quite frankly, rather careless assertion about a very complex issue. The concept of original sin is useful only to the degree that it helps us understand the impact of human sin on God's ability to maintain his relationship with humanity and with all of creation. Sin is no match for God's love. Sin is no match for God's grace. Sin is no match for God's blessing, which he has pronounced over creation upon the completion of his work.

I believe initial sin is a much better descriptor of what we see in the garden story, because initial sin isn't the cause of human disability. I do not believe that disability is the result of humanity's fall or sin. In fact, when we read the story of initial sin in Genesis, we actually see God's response. When humans choose to consume fruit from the forbidden tree, God confronts them and delivers the resulting consequences for the action. God curses the serpent (Gen. 3:14), makes childbirth and marriage more challenging (v. 16), and curses the ground (v. 17). God never curses humans as a result of their choice to consume the fruit.

What we do see, however, is the beginning of an adversarial relationship with the human body. When Adam and Eve give in to their desire for the fruit, their eyes are opened to a world that has already existed, and as a result, they become ashamed of their own bodies (Gen. 3:7). What would drive them to suddenly become ashamed of their bodies? Nothing changes externally. The world as they know it is still the same. The animals don't change. The environment doesn't change. Eating the fruit doesn't suddenly and subtly transform the world around them into a place they don't recognize. In fact, the idea that both God and the serpent discuss death as a consequence for eating the fruit suggests that humanity is very aware of the concept of death. Being told that death is a consequence of consuming the fruit would not have been a foreign idea to them. We don't present consequences that are unfamiliar to those receiving them. In order for a consequence to hold weight, a person must have some foreknowledge or experience with it.

The idea of human limitation is not foreign to humanity. Humans understand that the world they inhabit includes the reality that human bodies have limitations. Adam and Eve are just as naked before they eat the fruit (Gen. 2:25) as they are afterward. What that means as it relates to disability is that we must interrogate why we have the felt need to explain away human limitation by insisting that sin has transported us into a world where human bodies are cursed with imperfection. I don't believe the events of the garden story support this idea. What we do see, however, is the entrance of shame and its direct relationship to the human body. Shame is a central idea in the grand story about sin, God, and the human experience.

Death, human limitation, and even the serpent are all part of God's creative genius. Each is designed to play a role in God's ideal environment for human flourishing. The reality of all three of these is not foreign to human understanding. What is foreign to human understanding and to the human experience is shame. This is why God inquires about the source of Adam and Eve's shame. What causes them to suddenly be self-conscious about their nakedness? More important, what role does sin play in the subsequent shame humans experience over how their bodies look or function?

For Christians in the West, original sin means that humanity has a nature that is opposed to God. As a result, many Christians believe that we are deeply depraved and utterly incapable of any good. Sin is our natural state, and we are desperately in need of being rescued from our sinful nature. I can agree that humans are sinful. I can agree that we are all at our core selfish and self-serving beings. But there are also many theologians and scholars who contend that original sin does not necessarily imply that humans are incapable of doing good. Pastor, author, and theologian Danielle Shroyer writes in her book *Original Blessing*, "Of the three Abrahamic religions, only Christianity has a doctrine of original sin, and Christianity has never held this doctrine universally. Though it may seem that original sin is a given, Christian history tells us a different story. None of the Eastern branches of our family tree (Eastern Orthodox, Greek Orthodox, Armenian Christian) have ever accepted it, and of course our Jewish forbears, without who we would not have our tradition, have roundly and consistently rejected it."[1]

When given the choice, we have the tendency to choose our own desires over God's; after all, it is who we are as created beings. We cherish our freedom to choose, and yet a proclivity to pursue our own interests does not necessarily equate to a humanity being cursed with disability. If disability or human limitation were truly a consequence of the fall of humanity, then no one should be able to escape being born disabled. The idea that disability is a result of original sin lacks a consistency that can be observed by studying the sociological data on disability. Shroyer writes, "From a strict numbers perspective, the notion of a whole world full of people literally hell-bent on doing evil doesn't add up."[2]

Disabled people are the largest minority group in the world, but they are still a minority group. Certainly, if disability was a definite consequence of sin, then these numbers would be greater.

Still, some may argue that disability is a result of the fall. In other words, sin has made a perfect world imperfect, thus allowing for the possibility of people being born with abnormalities. This approach would help explain why every person born after the fall is not born disabled. Except this argument also lacks consistency because it still assumes that God has cursed human bodies and that the curse is completely random in its impact. It also makes the faulty assumption that a perfect world is a world in which disability and sickness do not exist. How, then, do we reconcile Adam and Eve being familiar with the concept of death, especially if God uses it as a deterrent for disobeying his command? Is it possible, after reading the list of consequences straight from God regarding humanity's sin, that we still want to believe that disability is a curse from God because we read the text through an ableist lens? If so, where should we shift our focus if we intend to address ableism and racism? How do we understand the role of joy in this work? The first step is what I call a decentering of our faith.

Developing a Decentering Faith

Over the last several years, the term *deconstruction* has been used to describe people leaving White evangelicalism. Scores of self-identifying evangelical Christians, both young and old, have declared themselves to be in the deconstruction phase of their faith journey. Most often, *deconstruction* refers to the rigid and rigorous interrogation of previously held beliefs related to Christian history, doctrine, and biblical interpretation. When deconstruction takes place, almost everything is placed on the chopping block. Deconstructionists have argued that large portions of Christian practice in the West are deeply troubling and often perpetuate systems of injustice rather than dismantle them. Deconstruction is the process of questioning the validity of the biblical text as a historically accurate book and, at the same time, questioning the use of the text.

While I understand the concept of deconstruction, as a disabled pastor, as someone who has often lived on the margins of mainstream Christianity, I see deconstruction as primarily a privilege for those who have access to power. Deconstruction is an inside job. More often than not, deconstruction—both the process and the final product, whatever that may be—doesn't come at a high cost for true insiders. While the perception of being an outsider is often perpetuated, we have to understand that deconstruction and the associated labeling of oneself as marginalized have become a way of shifting power within evangelical Christianity. There are entire movements surrounding deconstruction mainly because being an outsider has now become an advantage.

Deconstruction has its place, but I believe that, in the end, deconstruction falls short of its ultimate agenda because it masters the art of calling out people and practices without an obligation to call people in. Deconstruction shrinks the circle. It's the equivalent of theological musical chairs, going in circles until only one seat is left and one perspective is king. Deconstruction often doesn't leave enough seats at the table to expand our ideas about God. I believe that in order to grow in our understanding of God, we need to add to our knowledge base, not simply destroy it and leave it smoldering from the ashes of our raging anger. In addition to deconstruction, disability theology offers an opportunity for decentering our faith.

Decentering faith is an expansion project, not a demolition project. Decentering requires an intentional interrogation of Western Christianity by expanding our knowledge base. An expansion of our knowledge base means that we hold to the past narratives about faith, God, and the biblical text so that we can place them in conversation with narratives that have previously been excluded from the Christian canon. In this way, we can properly examine all of the available knowledge and experience about God and faith and engage in meaningful faith construction.

A central issue in discussions about disability is the question of design. So much of the Christian understanding of humanity is dependent on the understanding of design or origin. For many, the question of God's original design for the human body serves as the guide for their attempts at engaging disability, chronic illness, and human limitation. A belief that God has designed the human body to have one look, one function, and one experience is what anchors the theology of many people who oppose disability theology.

In their view, God has designed the human body to have a singular presentation, and anything that deviates even slightly from that original design is disabled or abnormal. It is important to note that not everyone who holds this view attributes disability or bodily abnormality to personal sin, yet many still do believe that the presence of bodily variation is a result of sin entering the world. There are two places in Scripture that I often turn to in order to challenge this idea. The first is a story in the Gospel of John, which goes as follows:

> As Jesus was walking along, he saw a man who had been blind from birth.
> "Rabbi," his disciples asked him, "why was this man born blind? Was it because of his own sins or his parents' sins?"
> "It was not because of his sins or his parents' sins," Jesus answered. "This happened so the power of God could be seen in him." (John 9:1–3)

Questions about the origins of disability or about the design of the human body aren't new. Even the earliest followers of Jesus held the perspective that disability must have been the result of sin—either original sin, passed down from our predecessors, or personal sin. The question about why this man was born blind actually isn't the best question to ask about disability. Jesus highlights this when he points his disciples to a third option for discussing disability.

Honestly, the question about disability and sin is a tragically common question even in our current context. But how often do we really stop to analyze why this question matters so much to us? I mean, how much could a child in utero have sinned in order to be born with a visual impairment? It doesn't make a lot of sense to assume that personal sin results in congenital disabilities. The other reason that this line of questioning is both awful and archaic is because it doesn't help explain other types of disabilities, such as age-related disabilities, disabilities like mine that are a result of a serious illness like cancer, or unfortunate accidents that lead to things such as traumatic brain injuries. How do we place sin into the conversation when a person becomes disabled due to life's circumstances? There aren't many answers to this question that are both thoughtful and helpful in assisting the disability community with the challenge of faith and life with a disability.

When Jesus answers his followers, I like to believe that he is also in conversation with historical views about disability, sin, and God's role in disability, at least congenital disabilities. Jesus provides a much more helpful answer. He denies that sin is the cause of the man's congenital blindness and instead points to God's role in the disability discussion. In Jesus's response, we see that disability is not the result of a human hereditary condition of sin. In other words, his disability has not been passed on to him because his parents are sinners. Now, this doesn't mean that his parents have not sinned. All humans sin. What it does mean is that disability is not a consequence of someone else's sin, which means that the idea of original sin being the cause of disability lacks sufficient merit. There is no curse on human bodies that potentiates congenital disability from generation to generation. In Genesis, God curses the snake and the soil, not Adam and Eve's seed. Disability is not a virus that passes from person to person.

In addition, Jesus is clear that it is not the blind man's personal sin that has caused his blindness. Even if it were possible for a child in the womb to sin against God, it still would not explain why he was born with a disability. In saying this, Jesus slams the door on the conversation about sin resulting in disability. Whatever historical view the disciples hold about the correlation between sin and disability is instantly shattered by Jesus's response. The story of human disability is not about sin. It never has been.

The second biblical text that I often turn to is the call narrative of Moses. In this story, God is calling Moses to participate in the liberation of the Hebrew people from Egyptian oppression. Moses, who is hiding out on the back side of a desert, encounters a burning bush that God uses to gain his attention. In one of the most interesting interactions recorded in the Bible, God seems to take responsibility for what Moses describes as a disability that affects his speech. "But Moses pleaded with the LORD, 'O Lord, I'm not very good with words. I never have been, and I'm not now, even though you have spoken to me. I get tongue-tied, and my words get tangled.' Then the LORD asked Moses, 'Who makes a person's mouth? Who decides whether people speak or do not speak, hear or do not hear, see or do not see? Is it not I, the LORD?'" (Exod. 4:10–11).

This startling revelation about God's role in disability is often overlooked or dismissed, particularly as it relates to the discussion of human design. Admittedly, I once struggled with the notion that God would take responsibility for actually creating a human being with a congenital disability.

What kind of God would create a person with the inability to speak or to walk or to see? This picture of God can be difficult to comprehend and to accept, but I believe that the overarching principle is that God is the author of human design, and we are woefully inexperienced in being able to determine what God's design for the human body actually is. If nothing else, God taking responsibility for creating people with disabilities certainly complicates our discussions about design.

A decentering faith requires us to acknowledge this complication, all while pursuing a broader understanding about God's role in disability and the concept of creative design. One of the most helpful tools in this pursuit is an expansion of our sample size, a look at creation beyond humanity. As humans, we tend to believe that we alone are the sole reflection of God's creative genius. Our sense of design is limited by our preoccupation with ourselves as the center of creation. However, nothing can be further from the truth. Humanity is not the sole reflection of God's creative genius, and for what it's worth, humanity is only a small sample size of what God creates.

Science is a wonderful tool in developing a decentering faith because it helps us discover the variety of ways in which God creates. For example, ostriches, penguins, turkeys, and chickens are all considered flightless birds. In fact, there are approximately sixty living species of birds that cannot fly. While science suggests that these birds have become flightless through evolution, there is still no consensus as to how this has actually happened. Almost all birds share the same type of anatomy; however, flightless birds share some common traits that show variations in bird anatomy. In the absence of the ability to fly, flightless birds have developed other attributes that have secured their survival from predators, such as an ability to swim or run at accelerated speeds.[3] What's most important as it relates to the conversation about design is the acknowledgment that millions of birds are born with wings that do not fulfill the purpose of their design.

There are several other ways science can help decenter our discussion about divine design. While there are several other species of animals that follow similar patterns as flightless birds, such as mammals who live under water, the creation narrative itself suggests that humanity is not the sole reflection of God's divine intellect. When we consider the placement of humanity into an already-existing environment, we have to seriously consider how the environment itself is a form of accommodation provided for human flourishing. Consider the way in which oxygen is provided through creation, as well as the way that gravity makes human mobility possible. Careful consideration of these scientific realities points to the interdependent nature of God's creation. Simply put, despite our best efforts to convince ourselves, independence is not an element of human design. We are utterly dependent on several accommodations that God has provided in his creation of the world. Perhaps this is why humanity was created last. In many ways, out of all of the living things God has created, humans are perhaps the most dependent. Unlike other mammals, humans are born with limited mobility, and we must age into some form of independence while also aging toward utter dependence. Decentering faith seeks to include the sum total of God's creative work and to include it in the discussion of dependence, independence, disability, ability, and design. When we realize humans are but a small part of the design discussion, we become far less certain of our understanding of what it means to be able-bodied.

Destroying Our Idols

Ableism reared its ugly head at the beginning of the global pandemic in 2020 through the vehicle of shame. We all know that the pandemic exposed inequities in our health-care system when it came to disproportionate numbers of people of color, people with disabilities, and elderly people dying from COVID-19. But ableism also exposed itself through shaming people into unhealthy pursuits of increased productivity.

Social media flooded with messages and memes suggesting that if people did not somehow use the time away from in-person activities to find new hobbies, form new side hustles, or finish home improvement projects, then they were utter failures. We were told to write books, create new products, start new podcasts, and develop merchandise, all while doing our very best to stay alive. The gospel of grind was in full effect, but even more than that, the use of shame as a motivator for productivity clouded our collective minds with pursuits that led us to mishandle such an important moment. Amid uncertainty about the severity of the virus, economic turmoil, and the mental health crisis, shame was used in ways that have been familiar to the disability community for some time. Shame was used to erect a new model idol of productivity.

Earlier in this chapter, I revisited the first of the three elements of bias by offering a way to address initial sin. In the same way that Micah in the book of Judges commits an initial sin that produces idols, so has the initial sin of ableism produced a deeply embedded idolatry for productivity. Remember that Micah seeks to avoid the shame of being cursed because of his sin, and while the response to the initial sin of American Christianity may be slightly different than Micah's, the result is still the same. That result is the creation of idols that are powered by the use of shame.

In her book *Daring Greatly: How the Courage to Be Vulnerable Transforms the Way We Live, Love, Parent, and Lead*, Brené Brown offers the following definition of shame:

> First, shame is the fear of disconnection. We are psychologically, emotionally, cognitively, and spiritually hardwired for connection, love, and belonging. Connection, along with love and belonging (two expressions of connection), is why we are here, and it is what gives purpose and meaning to our lives. Shame is the fear of disconnection—it's the fear that something we've done or failed to do, an ideal that we've not lived up to, or a goal that we've not accomplished makes us unworthy of connection. *I'm not worthy or good enough for love, belonging, or connection. I'm unlovable. I don't belong.* Here's the definition of shame that emerged from my research: *Shame is the intensely painful feeling or experience of believing that we are flawed and therefore unworthy of love and belonging.*[4]

Brown goes on to list twelve shame categories that emerged in her research, and it is not surprising that all of those categories, including religion, are directly connected to the body and its ability to produce or function in a certain way.

The question you may be asking at this point is this: What do idols have to do with shame? Idols stand as stark reminders of an ideal that is to be worshiped. Idolatry at its core is the deifying of standards, standards that are always used to represent the ideal behavior, the ideal bodies, the ideal beliefs, and the ideal benefits of declaring our allegiance to the idols we create. Idols become sacred because we make them holy. We make them highly sought-after images of social and spiritual status, at the expense of those we push out into the margins in the process.

Shame can be perpetuated in close proximity with others. We see the use of shame all the time in the way we operate in our own interpersonal relationships. Employers shame employees for not being able to live up to an ideal image. One of the ways we see this is when an employee shows up to work with an illness so as to not disappoint their employer. This also often happens in the school system when children are rewarded for perfect attendance. Parents also use shame when they set up idols and ideals for their children based on their perception of how their peers' children perform. Like racism, shame (and ableism) is definitely demonstrated on a personal level, but dismantling its use and the way that it powers ableist idols and images means that we also have to acknowledge that it is systemic. Shame not only produces a network of idols and images that promote both ableism and racism; it is also very often one of the most effective tools of the state.

State-sponsored shame is not a topic often connected to theological discussions, especially in relation to topics such as disability; however, systemic shame has long been a tool of the state to control perceptions of human ability. One of the most prominent and most current uses of shame as a state-sponsored tool is the lack of marriage equality for disabled people. While it is not technically illegal for disabled people to marry, a number of considerable barriers keep them from doing so without loss of social security, Medicaid, and Medicare benefits. Many people refer to these restrictions as marriage penalties. Disabled people who want to marry face the prospect of losing life-saving benefits, unless they marry someone who is also disabled. "Benefits and health care programs for disabled people tend to trap them in poverty in many ways, all of which could be changed to encourage work, marriage, and other aspects of a normal, stable, and rewarding life."[5] In addition, the rules support injustice against disabled people and punish them for attempting to ascend to what Western society has championed as the foundation of our culture, which is the family.

Creating barriers for disabled people to marry nondisabled people is one of the most sinister ways that our society uses state-sponsored shame to keep the idols of marriage, relationships, and even procreation limited to the able-bodied. The fact that disabled people are systematically encouraged to only marry other disabled people without the threat of losing health benefits is an example of the creation of an idol of success and stability that is powered by the shame of poverty. Marriage penalties shame disabled people into remaining unmarried by threatening them with poverty and, in very extreme cases, death. The good news is that when we reflect theologically about state-sponsored uses of shame that help to perpetuate both ableism and racism, we find that Jesus is intimately familiar with the use of state-sponsored shame as a tool of intimidation and control. The writer of Hebrews gives us a glimpse into how we can begin to dismantle shame and the hurtful idols and images that it supports by reminding us how Jesus approached his crucifixion. "Because of the joy awaiting him, he endured the cross, disregarding its shame. Now he is seated in the place of honor beside God's throne" (Heb. 12:2).

Toi Derricotte, a poet born in 1941 in Hamtramck, Michigan, once penned a line in her poetry about joy being an act of resistance. In an interview, she shared that she felt as a Black woman that her "sins" were confusing. "As a black woman, I have been consistently confused about my 'sins,' unsure of which faults were in me and which faults were the results of others' projections."[6] Derricotte believes that her work as an artist and poet has served as a necessary tool for separating herself from stereotypes about Black women.

Joy as an act of resistance is the use of the beauty of joy and the creativity of God to resist the unnecessary and unholy idols of Western Christianity. When the writer of Hebrews speaks about Jesus's relationship to the cross, he uses the word "joy" very intentionally as the chosen weapon of resistance to the type of state-sponsored shame that Roman crucifixion has been designed to create. Jesus, because of joy, has disregarded or dismantled the shame of the cross. What seems like such an insignificant statement is perhaps one of the most transformative understandings of the spiritual power to dismantle the idols of ableism and subsequently racism and all of the images they use, by resisting the shame of being considered abnormal or subhuman. In this way, joy is an act of resisting shame and the use of shame as an instrument of control. Joy is rebelling against wrong motives, underhanded agendas, and unjust practices. Joy resists darkness. Joy is an idol smasher.

Earlier in this book, we discussed one of the most critical tenets of disability theology—the concept of the disabled God, which was popularized by the late Nancy Eiesland. The primary reason for spending so much time unpacking Eiesland's theology was to help us understand the necessity of new imagery in Western Christianity. Jesus, the disabled God, disregards and dismantles the shame of the cross by ultimately providing us with a startling new image of a holy God with holes in his body. This new image is only as powerful as our willing acknowledgment that the goal of both the torture and the death of Jesus by the Roman government was to publicly shame him and his followers. In a holy, joy-filled, and supernaturally creative reversal of shame, the postresurrection body of Jesus retains the holes in his body and, in doing so, dismantles any attempts to use physical and spiritual shame as a foundation for creating idols and images that misrepresent God. Jesus uses the joy of his return and the retention of his disabled body as the way to eternally destroy the power of shame and the idols and images that it creates, especially the shame that was cast onto the human body as a result of the initial sin in the story of Eden.

So what would justice look like as we dismantle shame and the idols and images it creates, which so often fuel ableism and racism in Western Christianity? If justice is the leveling of the playing field and the reversal of unrighteous images and idols, then we can look closely at the standardized images of ableism and the privileges that are attached to ableist practices. A better question may be, How do we dismantle the image that able-bodiedness equals goodness and that Black bodies are inherently disabled?

Jesus once told a compelling story that provides us with a practical runway for the work of disability and racial justice. We know the story as that of the good Samaritan, a story in which Jesus questions our understanding of what it means to be a neighbor. In the story, a man is beaten and left for dead. He is no doubt at least temporarily disabled due to the circumstances of traveling the road and his encounter with dangerous robbers and thieves. While we often pay keen attention to the response of the Samaritan, we should also pay close attention to the priest and the Levite in the story. What motivates their passing of the disabled man is more than just a religious duty and commitment to not render themselves unclean and unable to serve their faith community.

What we witness in the story of the good Samaritan is the privilege that ableism creates for those who are not designated as disabled. The priest and the Levite are not necessarily bad people. They are privileged people. They know that failing to stop to help the temporarily disabled man would not jeopardize their standing in society or in the faith community. In other words, their image is protected. They do not have to change the way they see the man in order to maintain their status as good people. In my book *Disability and the Church: A Vision for Diversity and Inclusion*, I make a simple statement that is at the heart of our challenge for true justice and the dismantling of ableism in Western Christianity. Western Christianity has taught us how to be "good people" without actually having to be good to people.[7] This is what the priest and Levite know well. They can still maintain their image of being good people in the community and in the synagogues and not have to change their views about people or the practices of their faith community. Sadly, Western Christianity has taught us the same. Ableism continues to exist, and it continues to fuel racism and other forms of discrimination because we have created a privileged and protected status that does not require us to practice justice in order to still consider ourselves good people or God's people. In order to destroy ableism, we must destroy the privilege and the protection that comes with it. We must be willing to see ourselves as Jesus sees us—people who are unwilling to be neighbors yet who are unwilling to see ourselves as anything but the heroes we continually pretend to be.

Better Imagination and Broader Inspiration

Initial sin. Images and idols. Institutions. What, then, do we do about change? First, nothing changes in our institutions until we dismantle the idols and images that ableism has created. Just as Micah creates an institution around the images and idols both he and his mother create, so has the Western church created an institution around ableist and racist images and idols. Dismantling ableism begins with reimagining the relevance of current institutions on the front lines that are addressing systemic injustices around the globe. Let's be honest: before we attempt to create new institutions to battle against ableism in the church, we first have to return to the discussion of how ableism has already disregarded the bodies of work being produced by organizations and groups that are often labeled as unchristian. The Western church has long believed that it has a monopoly on what is Christian and what constitutes justice; however, history has shown that we have had the tendency to be wrong. In our discussion about the role of the Black church, we discovered that the historically Black church came about as a result of ableist and racist interpretations of what it meant to be Christian. Interpretations of Scripture, justice, and idolatry that have led the Western church away from its ableist and racist idols came from the very institution that the White Western church has ostracized and labeled as doctrinally incorrect. Down the road, I'd like to write more about the importance of the historically Black church in the movement to dismantle ableism, but for now, I believe our best resources as a church will come from not only the historically Black church but many other institutions that the church has dismissed. The overarching theme in the book of Judges, including the end of Micah's story, is that people did what was right "in their own eyes."

This is why it is absolutely critical that the church consider the brilliance and beauty of institutions that are creatively wrestling with the challenges of understanding the human body, disability and ability, and the creation of race as a social construct and as a social standing in Western civilization. If we are to be faithful to our call to justice, we must be willing to decenter ourselves as the source for all knowledge and wisdom on these topics. The Western church has done what has been right in its own eyes, and it has led us to a warped sense of what following Jesus should look like. The church has a chance to recalibrate, but it will absolutely require a commitment to reduce the use of our own perspective and increase the input of those whom ableism, racism, and other forms of discrimination have pushed to the margins. Our task is not an easy one, but it is one that is achievable through the power of God's Spirit. Jesus has promised to build his church, and with that promise has come an assurance that the very gates of hell will be unsuccessful in trying to dismantle and destroy his work. The Western church is not without her share of flaws, but she is also not outside the promise of prevailing against the foes of her faith. Ableism is evil, but it is not eternal. By contrast, God's church is eternal.

NOTES

Introduction

1. For a more detailed account of this incident, see Lamar Hardwick, "Fear, Faith, Philando and How the Church Is Failing," Autism Pastor, June 22, 2017, https://autismpastor.com/?p=2168.

2. Nicquel Terry Ellis, Martin Savidge, and Angela Barajas, "Ahmaud Arbery's Death Sparked Some Policy Change, but One Year Later His Family Still Awaits Justice," CNN, last updated February 23, 2021, https://www.cnn.com/2021/02/23/us/ahmaud-arbery-one-year-anniversary/index.html.

3. Lucy Tompkins, "Here's What You Need to Know about Elijah McClain's Death," New York Times, January 18, 2022, www.nytimes.com/article/who-was-elijah-mcclain.html.

4. Omar Jimenez, Amir Vera, and Eric Levenson, "Elijah McClain's Mother Relieved He 'Is No Longer Labeled a Suspect' after Investigation into Officers' Actions," CNN, last updated February 22, 2021, https://edition.cnn.com/2021/02/22/us/elijah-mcclain-aurora-police-death/index.html.

5. Charles M. Blow, "The Bias against Black Bodies," New York Times, February 20, 2014, https://www.nytimes.com/2014/02/20/opinion/the-bias-against-black-bodies.html.

6. Patricia G. Devine, "Stereotypes and Prejudice: Their Automatic and Controlled Components," Journal of Personality and Social Psychology 56, no. 1 (1989): 5–18, https://doi.org/10.1037/0022-3514.56.1.5.

7. G. W. Allport and L. J. Postman, "The Psychology of Rumor," Journal of Clinical Psychology 3, no. 4 (1947): 247.

Chapter 1 Disability, Blackness, and Early American Christianity

1. "42 U.S. Code § 12102—Definition of Disability," Legal Information Institute, Cornell Law School, https://www.law.cornell.edu/uscode /text/42/12102.

2. Kim E. Nielsen, *A Disability History of the United States*, ReVisioning American History (Boston: Beacon, 2012), 12.

3. The term *retardation* is no longer used and is now referred to as *intellectual disability*.

4. H. Rutherford Turnbull III, "'Free at Last': Kennedy, King, and the Meaning of Liberty in the Disability Rights Movement," *Research and Practice for Persons with Severe Disabilities* 37, no. 3 (2012): 211, https://doi.org/10.2511/027494812804153543.

5. Turnbull, "'Free at Last,'" 211.

6. Clayborne Carson and Peter Holloran, eds., *A Knock at Midnight: Inspiration from the Great Sermons of Reverend Martin Luther King, Jr.* (New York: Warner Books, 2000), 101.

Chapter 2 The Road to Racism

1. Isabel Wilkerson, *Caste: The Origins of Our Discontents* (New York: Random House, 2020), loc. 552, Kindle (emphasis added).

Chapter 3 John Piper and the Politics of Desirability

1. Lamar Hardwick, "A Letter from My Wife on the 1st Anniversary of My Autism Diagnosis," Autism Pastor, July 1, 2016, https://autism pastor.com/?p=1364.

2. "About Us," Desiring God, December 3, 2021, www.desiringgod .org/about-us.

3. John Piper, "Why Did God Make Me Unattractive?," Desiring God, November 1, 2021, https://www.desiringgod.org/interviews/why -did-god-make-me-unattractive (emphasis added).

4. Da'Shaun L. Harrison, *Belly of the Beast: The Politics of Anti-Fatness as Anti-Blackness* (Berkeley: North Atlantic Books, 2021), 13.

5. Piper, "Why Did God Make Me Unattractive?"

6. Susan M. Schweik, *The Ugly Laws: Disability in Public*, History of Disability (New York: New York University Press, 2009), 26.

7. Ela Przybylo and Sara Rodrigues, "Introduction: On the Politics of Ugliness," in *On the Politics of Ugliness*, ed. Sara Rodrigues and Ela Przybylo (Toronto: Palgrave Macmillan, 2018), 17.

8. Schweik, *Ugly Laws*, 50–51.

Chapter 4 Do No Harm

1. Heather H. Vacek, *Madness: American Protestant Responses to Mental Illness*, Studies in Religion, Theology, and Disability (Waco: Baylor University Press, 2015), 17.

2. Vacek, *Madness*, 10.

3. Sabrina Strings, *Fearing the Black Body: The Racial Origins of Fat Phobia* (New York: New York University Press, 2019), 169.

4. Tiffany Kindre, "ACPE Brief History," ACPE, accessed May 27, 2022, https://acpe.edu/docs/default-source/acpe-history/acpe-brief -history.pdf?sfvrsn=a9e02b71_2.

5. Amanda D'Ambrosio, "Black Doctor Dies after Giving Birth, Underscoring Maternal Mortality Crisis," MedPage Today, November 2, 2020, https://www.medpagetoday.com/obgyn/pregnancy/89462.

6. "Preeclampsia," Cleveland Clinic, accessed May 24, 2022, https:// my.clevelandclinic.org/health/diseases/17952-preeclampsia.

7. D'Ambrosio, "Black Doctor Dies after Giving Birth."

8. Joelle Goldstein, "'Beloved' Pediatrics Doctor Dies from Postpartum Complications after Giving Birth to First Child," PEOPLE.com, November 6, 2020, https://www.people.com/human-interest/indiana -doctor-dies-from-postpartum-complications-after-giving-birth-first -child.

9. D'Ambrosio, "Black Doctor Dies after Giving Birth."

10. Nina Martin, ProPublica, and Renee Montagne, "Black Mothers Keep Dying after Giving Birth. Shalon Irving's Story Explains Why," NPR, December 7, 2017, https://www.npr.org/2017/12/07/568948782 /black-mothers-keep-dying-after-giving-birth-shalon-irvings-story -explains-why?t=1686669557095.

11. Vacek, *Madness*.

12. Nada Hassanein, "For Black Americans, Lack of 'Rigorous Scientific Evidence' Led to Test That Leaves Some Off Kidney Transplant List," USA Today, last updated October 13, 2021, https://www.usatoday.com /story/news/health/2021/10/13/black-americans-egfr-kidney-test -affects-ransplant-patients/6035288001/.

13. Hassanein, "For Black Americans."

14. Quoted in Hassanein, "For Black Americans."

15. Strings, *Fearing the Black Body*.

16. Sonya Renee Taylor, *The Body Is Not an Apology: The Power of Radical Self-Love*, 2nd ed. (Oakland: Berrett-Koehler, 2021), 24.

17. Régine Michelle Jean-Charles, *Martin Luther King and "The Trumpet of Conscience" Today* (Maryknoll, NY: Orbis Books, 2021), 123.

18. Tina Suliman, "Black Maternal Mortality: 'It Is Racism, Not Race,'" Johns Hopkins Center for Communication Programs, May 17, 2021, https://ccp.jhu.edu/2021/05/17/maternal-mortality-black-mamas -race-momnibus/.

19. "Racism and Health," Centers for Disease Control and Prevention, last reviewed November 24, 2021, https://www.cdc.gov/minority health/racism-disparities/index.html.

20. Nikole Hannah-Jones, Caitlin Roper, Ilena Silverman, and Jake Silverstein, eds., *The 1619 Project: A New Origin Story* (New York: One World, 2021), 315–17.

Chapter 5 Blackballed

1. Leonardo Blair, "Eric Mason Calls James White 'Racist' for Calling Black Churches 'Especially' Theologically Unsound," *Christian Post*, November 10, 2019, https://www.christianpost.com/news/eric-mason-calls -bible-expert-james-white-racist-for-calling-black-churches-especially -theologically-unsound.html.

2. Blair, "Eric Mason Calls James White 'Racist.'"

3. Henry Louis Gates Jr., *The Black Church: This Is Our Story, This Is Our Song* (New York: Penguin Press, 2021), 46–47.

4. Gates, *Black Church*, 64.

Chapter 6 The Disabled God and the Rise of the American Jesus

1. Nancy L. Eiesland, *The Disabled God: Toward a Liberatory Theology of Disability* (Nashville: Abingdon, 1994), 95.

2. Eiesland, *Disabled God*, 99.

Chapter 7 Bodies of Work

1. Gus Alexiou, "Remote Work Boosts Employees with Disabilities, Research Shows," *Forbes*, October 27, 2022, https://www.forbes.com /sites/gusalexiou/2022/10/27/new-research-confirms-boon-of-re mote-working-for-disabled-employees-in-the-us/?sh=5da60ab05aa4.

2. Rachel Marie Kang, *Let There Be Art: The Pleasure and Purpose of Unleashing the Creativity within You* (Grand Rapids: Revell, 2022), 23.

3. Jeffery M. Leonard, *Creation Rediscovered: Finding New Meaning in an Ancient Story* (Peabody, MA: Hendrickson Academic, 2020), 165.

Chapter 8 Disability, the Cross, and Unraveling Shame

1. Jemar Tisby, *The Color of Compromise: The Truth about the American Church's Complicity in Racism* (Grand Rapids: Zondervan, 2020), 39.

2. Esau McCaulley, *Reading While Black: African American Biblical Interpretation as an Exercise in Hope* (Downers Grove, IL: IVP Academic, 2020), 17.

3. McCaulley, *Reading While Black*, 107.

4. James H. Cone, *The Cross and the Lynching Tree* (Maryknoll, NY: Orbis Books, 2011), 3.

5. See Willie James Jennings, "Gathering Joy," Yale Center for Faith & Culture, YouTube, December 20, 2018, https://www.youtube.com/watch?v=7jGG5ZtABH0.

Conclusion

1. Danielle Shroyer, *Original Blessing: Putting Sin in Its Rightful Place* (Minneapolis: Fortress, 2016), 25–26.

2. Shroyer, *Original Blessing*, 30.

3. Melissa Mayntz, "Flightless Birds: List of Species around the World," Spruce, last updated August 28, 2022, https://www.thespruce.com/why-some-birds-dont-fly-385428.

4. Brené Brown, *Daring Greatly: How the Courage to Be Vulnerable Transforms the Way We Live, Love, Parent, and Lead* (New York: Avery, 2015), 68–69 (emphasis original).

5. Andrew Pulrang, "What's Next In 'Marriage Equality' for People with Disabilities?," Forbes, March 31, 2022, https://www.forbes.com/sites/andrewpulrang/2022/03/31/whats-next-in-marriage-equality-for-people-with-disabilities/.

6. "Toi Derricotte," Poetry Foundation, accessed January 26, 2023, https://www.poetryfoundation.org/poets/toi-derricotte.

7. Lamar Hardwick, *Disability and the Church: A Vision for Diversity and Inclusion* (Downers Grove, IL: InterVarsity Press, 2021), 73.

LAMAR HARDWICK (DMin, Liberty Baptist Theological Seminary) is the lead pastor of Tri-Cities Church in East Point, Georgia, and author of the books *Epic Church*, *I Am Strong: The Life and Journey of an Autistic Pastor*, and *Disability and the Church: A Vision for Diversity and Inclusion*.

In 2014, after years of silently struggling with social anxiety, sensory processing disorder, and a host of other significant issues, Hardwick was diagnosed with autism spectrum disorder at the age of thirty-six. He now offers workshops and seminars on autism and consults with local churches and faith-based organizations on creating environments for people with autism. He also provides mentoring services for teens and young adults on the autism spectrum. His writing has been published by The Mighty, *The Huffington Post*, Key Ministry, and The Autistic Self Advocacy Network.

He lives in Newnan, Georgia, with his wife, Isabella, and their three children.